D0933179

# *SEASONS OF THE*

# WHALE

# SEASONS OF THE

# WHALE

## Riding the Currents of the North Atlantic

## ERICH HOYT

Nimbus Publishing Limited

Copyright © 1990, 1997 by Erich Hoyt
All rights reserved.

Nimbus Publishing Limited
P.O. Box 9301, Station A
Halifax, Nova Scotia  B3K 5N5
(902) 455-4286

Design: Steven Slipp, GDA, Halifax, Nova Scotia
Printed in Hong Kong

Canadian Cataloguing in Publication Data
Hoyt, Erich, 1950–
Seasons of the whale
Includes bibliographical references and index.
ISBN 0-921054-52-1
ISBN 1-55109-226-3 (pbk)
I. Whales—North Atlantic Ocean.
2. Whales—North Atlantic Ocean—Pictorial works.
I. Title
QL737.C4H68    1990 599.5    C90-097575-X

# ACKNOWLEDGMENTS

This 1997 edition marks the ten-year anniversary of the events of this book and makes us acutely aware that there is much work yet to do to ensure a future for whales and dolphins in the seas around us.

For the first edition, I would like to thank Don Anderson, Lisa Baraff, Pierre Béland, Martine Bérubé, Carole Carlson, Phil Clapham, Charles Doucet, Dave Gaskin, Laurie Goldman, Jonathan Gordon, Amy Knowlton, Scott Kraus, Dotte Larsen, Jon Lien, Ken Mann, Daniel Martineau, Bruce McKay, Nancy Miller, Andrew Read, Bill Rossiter, Bob Schoelkopf, Mason Weinrich, Fred Wenzel, Alan White, Hal Whitehead, Mike Williamson, and especially Richard Sears, who helped initiate the project. Many of these people provided papers, private journals, ship logs, computer printouts of whale sightings, and photographs. They also granted interviews.

I am grateful to the publisher, Dorothy Blythe, editor, Nancy Robb, designer, Steven Slipp, production assistants, Leona Hachey and Dereck Day, and indexer, Robbie Rudnicki. Some of the ideas for this book grew out of discussions with Jane Holtz Kay, Murray Melbin, Judith Tick, and Cheryl Bentsen, at sessions of a writers' group, founded by Janice Harayda, that met in Boston between 1987 and 1989. Valuable comments, advice, and inspiration came from John Oliphant, Peter Vatcher, Mary Trokenberg, Sarah Wedden, and Robert Hoyt.

E.H.

TO SARAH AND MOSE,
*with tenderness for all seasons*

# CONTENTS

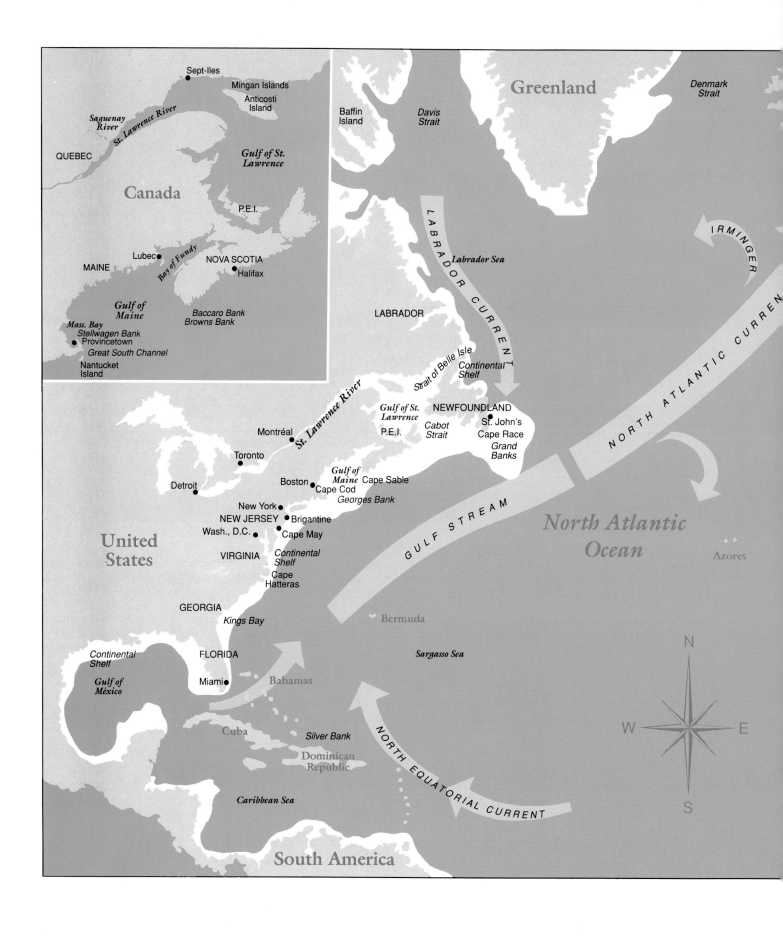

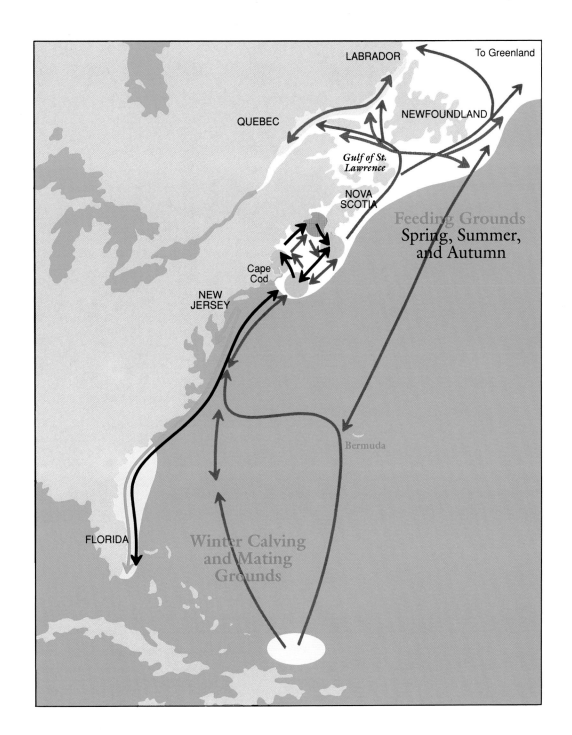

## Probable Migration Routes

— **Humpback Whales** ☐ Mating/Calving Grounds ☐ Feeding Grounds

— **Right Whales** ☐ Calving Grounds ☐ Feeding Grounds ☐ Nursery/Feeding Grounds

— **Blue Whales** ☐ Feeding Grounds

— **Bottlenose Dolphins**

PHOTOGRAPH: JANE GIBBS

# PREFACE

IN THE EPIC STORY of the North Atlantic Ocean, whales are tragic heroes. Five hundred years ago, when Columbus set sail for the New World, the North Atlantic was teeming with life—seals, sea birds, turtles, fish, dolphins, porpoises, and whales. That first trip was the start of an era of magic discovery. To stock subsequent voyages, sailors killed sea life for food, skins, furs, and other products. But as expedition sponsors grew rich, human greed prevailed. More than any other exploitable animal, the whale offered rewards on a grand scale. A single 50-ton right whale, for example, yielded 80 barrels of oil. Although prices fluctuated, the income from one large whale was often enough to finance a year of whaling. All the rest was profit.

As the explorers opened and mapped new areas, whaling spread from the shores of western Europe to Greenland, then to Massachusetts, Newfoundland, Nova Scotia, and other areas along the coast of North America. Over five centuries, whalers had their way in the North Atlantic, driving one whale species after another to near-extinction, before moving on to other seas. More than 90 percent of the humpback, right, and blue whales that originally filled all the seas on Earth are now gone. But in the vast world ocean, the whalers could not catch all of them. Some species, now that whaling has stopped for the most part, are even starting to recover.

Today in the North Atlantic, there are remnant populations of 15 species of whales, in addition to 15 species of dolphins and porpoises. I have chosen to follow humpback, blue, and right whales, mainly because they are the three most intensively studied whales in the North Atlantic. Except for the blue whale, which disappears for most of the winter and spring, they are the subjects of year-round research. In the modern drama of the North Atlantic, these three species have become central characters. Each, with some overlap, has its own kind of life, lives in or visits different regions, and encounters various obstacles, mostly human activities. Other species of whales and dolphins, of course, play important supporting roles, as do fishes, crustaceans, and plankton. Together, all these organisms, from microscopic plankton to whales, make up the ocean's food chain, the crucial link between predator and prey, without which life in the sea would collapse.

Although this is a non-fiction narrative, I have tried to write it from the point of view of wild whales. Whales and humans share certain experiences as mammals: both are dependent on their mothers for milk, comfort, and safety; both are air breathing; and both have developed complex, dynamic social groups. Fellow mammals such as humans can sense in their bones how a whale must feel in certain situations. Yet I have tried to tell the story without giving the whales human traits or motives. Keeping poetic license to a minimum, I have drawn instead on the long-term studies of whales in the wild. This is the truest picture of whales that we have.

The modern era of whale research began in the early 1970s, during the last days of whaling off North America. There were no longer enough whales to make whaling commercially profitable. Were there enough left to study? Many of the researchers were 1960s idealists who had joined the save-the-whales movement and then become interested in finding out more about these large-brained animals. Once they met whales at sea—whales that could sing and whose gravity-defying leaps were so full of power and grace—they became hooked. Their careful work over two decades has focused on individual animals that the researchers identify through natural markings on the back, head, or tail. They have given the whales names, charted year-to-year movements through the world ocean, and observed even the most intimate behavior. From these researchers' notes and journals, as well as from published papers, I have tried to reconstruct a year in the lives of about a dozen whales.

I have met most of the whales and dolphins that I talk about in this book. During hundreds of hours at sea in the North Atlantic, I have eaten whale food—fashioned into krill and copepod sandwiches, which taste a little like shrimp-paté sandwiches. In researchers' homes and offices, I have slept under the odd 10-foot-long whale jawbone, using a life jacket as a pillow. I have come to know and count as friends many of the whale researchers, an informal community of several hundred, mostly Canadians, Americans, and Britons. Many of them do not have formal degrees, as the science of studying whales is so new. And few have time to sit still! A whale researcher is always on the go, because a whale can travel 100 miles in a day and range over thousands of miles in a season. Many researchers try to monitor a species at both ends of the migration path. For most, that means summers in the Gulf of St. Lawrence, the Bay of Fundy, and the Gulf of Maine, then winters off Florida or in the Caribbean. When they are not at sea, they are running off to conferences or workshops, whale strandings, and the "naming-of-the-new-whales" party, held each spring in Provincetown, Massachusetts.

I chose the year 1987 in part because it was a momentous year for whales and whale researchers alike—a year when they drew closer than ever before. It was also the year when the health of the North Atlantic began to play a prominent role in the lives of both whales and humans. That summer, in seacoast towns and beach resorts from New England to Florida, the North Atlantic, having had enough, was returning some of what it had taken from us, without complaint, for years. All kinds of things were washing up, such as syringes and other medical waste. More things were washing up as well, including an unprecedented number of dead whales and dolphins. Surrounded by the carcasses of old whale friends, researchers were confronted with a painful irony. They had helped save the whales from whaling, but they had not saved the whales' habitat.

The whales' habitat stretches along their migration path, from the tropics, in most cases, to the cool temperate or polar zone. Whales need a route free from potentially hazardous fishing nets and traps. They need a certain amount of peace and quiet, especially in areas where they mate, and nurse their calves. They need a healthy environment for their food and for the plants and animals on which that food depends.

Whales are long-lived animals. When the older whales alive today were young, in the middle years of this century, they no doubt watched their mates fall, harpooned throughout the world ocean. It was a cruel death—cold steel pins penetrated blubber and splintered bone—and it destroyed many whale families. The whales we see today are the lucky older ones, and their progeny, who have survived to bear witness to the irony of the fouling of the sea.

Now, people pay to watch whales. Some of the old bulls, of course, remain wary and elusive, characteristics that once had survival value. Many more whales, however, mostly young cows and their calves, are greeting humans and making fast friends. In this close-up, eye-to-eye contact are the seeds of the whales' survival. If we can protect the whales' habitat in the North Atlantic—once the scene of death by harpoon and now the dump for the world's most industrial cities—that ocean may one day become a special place, a hallowed sea where humans and whales can meet.

*Erich Hoyt*
Edinburgh, Scotland

# CAST OF CHARACTERS

*Scene:* The North Atlantic Ocean

*Year:* 1987. It could be any year.

COMET, a male humpback whale
   (*Megaptera novaeangliae*)
TORCH, a male humpback whale
TALON, a female humpback whale
RUSH, Talon's calf, Sinestra's grandcalf
BELTANE, a female humpback whale
CAT EYES, Beltane's calf, Silver's grandcalf, a male
SILVER, Beltane's mother
SINESTRA, Talon's mother
POINT, a female humpback whale
CROW'S NEST, SHARK, NEW MOON, SCYLLA,
   PUMP, TATTERS, BISLASH, TUNING FORK,
   and other humpback whales from the Gulf of Maine
JIGSAW, a male humpback whale in the
   Gulf of St. Lawrence

STRIPE, a female right whale (*Eubalaena glacialis*)
STRIPE'S FIFTH CALF, a female
STARS, Stripe's third calf, a female
STARS'S CALF, Stripe's grandcalf
FOREVER, Stripe's fourth calf

JUNE, a female blue whale (*Balaenoptera musculus*)
JUNIOR, June's calf
COSMO, a blue whale that visits the Gulf of Maine
BACKBAR, KITS, PITA, PATCHES, HAGAR,
   BULLETA, and other favorite blue whales

CURLEY, a male fin whale (*Balaenoptera physalus*)

Sei whales (*Balaenoptera borealis*)
Minke whales (*Balaenoptera acutorostrata*)
Sperm whales (*Physeter macrocephalus*)
Pilot whales (*Globicephala melaena*)
Belugas, or white whales (*Delphinapterus leucas*)
Bottlenose dolphins (*Tursiops truncatus*)

Spinner dolphins (*Stenella longirostris*)
Atlantic spotted dolphins (*Stenella plagiodon*)
Atlantic white-sided dolphins (*Lagenorhynchus acutus*)
Harbor porpoises (*Phocoena phocoena*)
Harp seals (*Phoca groenlandica*)
Harbor seals (*Phoca vitulina concolor*)
Leatherback turtles (*Dermochelys coriacea*)
Loggerhead turtles (*Caretta caretta*)
Basking sharks (*Cetorhinus maximus*)
American sand lance (*Ammodytes americanus*)
Atlantic herring (*Clupea harengus*)
American plaice (*Hippoglossoides platessoides*)
Atlantic capelin (*Mallotus villosus*)
Atlantic cod (*Gadus morhua*)
Atlantic mackerel (*Scomber scombrus*)
Menhaden (*Brevoortia* species)
Squid (especially *Illex illecebrosus* and *Loligo* species)
Barnacles (especially *Coronula* and *Conchoderma* species)
Cyamids (*Cyamus* species)
Krill, or euphausiids (*Meganyctiphanes norvegica* and
   *Thysanoessa raschii*)
Copepods (especially *Calanus finmarchicus*)
Diatoms
Many million other zooplankton and phytoplankton

SCOTT KRAUS, a right-whale researcher
AMY KNOWLTON, a right-whale researcher
PHIL CLAPHAM, a humpback-whale researcher
CAROLE CARLSON, a humpback-whale researcher
LISA BARAFF, a humpback-whale researcher
JEFF GOODYEAR, a humpback-whale researcher
MASON WEINRICH, a humpback-whale researcher
MARTINE BERUBE, a blue-whale researcher
DIANE GENDRON, a blue-whale researcher
RICHARD SEARS, a blue-whale researcher
JON LIEN, a marine-mammal researcher
BOB SCHOELKOPF, a marine-mammal researcher
PIERRE BELAND, a beluga researcher
DANIEL MARTINEAU, a beluga researcher

BENEATH THE COVER OF THE WAVES
*and the wind, below the surface of the sea, there is a steady
humming punctuated by cries, brays, and whistles.
It is a special world, a world of sound.*

# WINTER

**A**S THE NORTHERN HEMISPHERE tilts away from the sun, the days become short, and the nights become long, darker than dark, and cold. Arctic winds blow over the Canadian Shield to the ice edge of Québec and Labrador. From there, the winds sweep across the mostly frozen Gulf of St. Lawrence to the rocky isle of Newfoundland and, farther south, bring an icy white winter to Nova Scotia, New Brunswick, and Maine. The North Atlantic Ocean in winter is damp, foggy, windy, alternately rainy or snowy, bone chilling, and cold. The foul-weather sailor or fisherman who falls overboard will die of exposure in minutes.

Yet only 200 miles offshore, the climate is gentler. Even in winter, the great Gulf Stream, driven by trade winds, carries warm water from the tropical Caribbean up along the coast of Florida, Georgia, and the Carolinas. Forced out to sea by a combination of the Earth's rotation and North Carolina's protruding outer coast, the Gulf Stream is carried even farther out

Icebergs off Greenland are driven south-ward by Arctic winds and surface currents.

PHOTOGRAPH: NORBERT WU

*Page 1:*
Pancake ice floes break up off Greenland.
PHOTOGRAPH: ERICH HOYT

by the continental rise south of the Grand Banks of Newfoundland. There, it becomes the North Atlantic Current and moves toward Britain, bearing the gifts of mild winters for northern Europe and of ice-free navigation as far north as the fjords of Norway near the Arctic Circle.

Meanwhile, New England and eastern Canada miss most of the warming from the Gulf Stream. Instead, icy surface water arrives from the Arctic Ocean, pouring through Davis Strait, along the west side of Greenland, into the Labrador Sea and the North Atlantic. Flowing beneath the Labrador Current—at intermediate and abyssal depths—is dense, cold water.

There are only four areas in the world where cold, deep water is formed, and the Labrador Sea is one of them. It happens when the extension of the Gulf Stream mixes with warmer, saltier water from the Mediterranean Sea that flows up near Labrador's ice edge in winter. As the cold, dry Arctic winds blow over the ice, the water cools rapidly, becomes very dense—much heavier than the water below—and sinks. One witness to this rare "deep-water formation" is physical oceanographer R. Allyn Clarke, of the Bedford Institute of Oceanography, in Dartmouth, Nova Scotia. He describes it as a vertical current, a river jetting to the bottom at up to 18 feet per second. Once on the bottom, the Labrador Sea deep water embarks on a 1,000-year trip around the world, creeping south along the Mid-Ocean Canyon of the North Atlantic. These and other deep waters, born in Arctic and Antarctic seas, cycle throughout the system, filling 70 percent of the world ocean. Thus, some of the water carried north-northeast in the Gulf Stream returns, maybe months or years later, considerably colder and denser and at abyssal depths. In future years, it will slowly move south through the North Atlantic, mix with other deep waters, cross the Equator, and twist around the southern

Beneath the frozen margins of the North Atlantic, even in midwinter, there is life. Harp seals, up to six feet long and weighing 400 pounds, perform ballets under the ice and dive deep for fish, returning often to the surface to keep their breathing holes open.

PHOTOGRAPH: TOM McCOLLUM, INTERNATIONAL FUND FOR ANIMAL WELFARE

tip of South America. Circulating throughout the world ocean system, this cold, deep water will end up—sometime after the year 3000—in the North Pacific, where some of it will once again enter the surface waters.

AS COLD AS IT IS ALONG NEWFOUNDLAND'S ICE EDGE—EVEN at the height of winter—there is life. Plankton continue to bloom, and swarms of krill and schools of fish gather to feed. This tempts some whales to remain in the area much longer than they should. Fish do not need to come to the surface to breathe, and seals can haul out on the ice if necessary. But whales get stuck. Every year, a few whales wait too long and get caught as the ice pushes in and breathing holes close over. Some die when the ice becomes too thick to break through. Even the huge blue whales—at up to 100 feet long the largest animal ever—sometimes take a chance and lose: the scars on the bodies of living blues attest to their ice battering. The "sensible" whales, of course, and the dolphins and the porpoises,  move far out to sea or depart

A humpback whale breaches—40 tons of flying muscle and blubber—and lands on its back. Humpbacks have decidedly reptilian profiles and carry large barnacle colonies that may weigh more than 1,000 pounds.

PHOTOGRAPH: WILLIAM ROSSITER

for southern latitudes. The sensible human researchers either go south to study whales, or hibernate in warm laboratories in cities such as Boston, Halifax, and Montréal to write papers on the summer's fieldwork.

Of all the migrating whales, humpbacks choose the most pleasant places for their winter holidays. In the North Pacific, they winter around Hawaii and coastal México. In the North Atlantic, after spending much of the spring, summer, and autumn off New England, Nova Scotia, Newfoundland, and Greenland, they can be found some 2,000 miles south, cavorting in the 80°F (25°C) water of the Caribbean. A favorite spot is around Silver Bank, a platform reef 60 miles north of the Dominican Republic.

The humpback whale's scientific name, *Megaptera novaeangliae*, means "great-winged creature of New England." Yankee whalers sometimes spotted humpbacks by their long white flippers: at up to 16 feet in length, they are the longest appendages in the animal kingdom. A breaching humpback whale, flippers outstretched, looks as if it might take flight or, when it turns on its side and offers a flipper to the wind, as if it might set sail, especially in the steady trade winds of the Caribbean.

And what a season for sailing! The waters of Silver Bank shimmer and sparkle in the sunlight. The name Silver Bank, however, does not come from the glistening waters but from the many silver-laden treasure ships that crashed on this barrier reef. Early mariners, busy counting their silver in ships weighted down to the gunnels, often lost everything. But for humpbacks, the reef offers a sheltered, protected environment from the sometimes nasty trade-wind swells. Here, humpbacks mate, give birth, and raise their calves. Winter after winter, they return.

A humpback mother rolls on her side to wave a flipper, and the calf follows suit. The white flippers of the humpback whale, up to 16 feet in length, are the longest appendages in the animal kingdom.
PHOTOGRAPH: WILLIAM ROSSITER

Researchers have befriended many of these humpbacks and have even given them names—Silver, Beltane, Bislash, Sinestra, Point, Cat Eyes, Talon, Rush, Comet, and Torch. Where do the names come from? Humpbacks flip their tails as they prepare to make a long dive, and every tail's underside has a different black-and-white pattern, ranging from nearly all black to nearly all white. This pattern, as unique as a snowflake, enables researchers to identify each humpback. The names come from patterns suggested by the tail markings or from other distinctive physical features. Comet, for example, has a white streak across the otherwise all-black underside of his tail. Another, Talon, has a white mark shaped like an "L"—resembling a bird's talon, or claw—on her flukes. Sometimes, however, a name comes from a whale's behavior or simply from a researcher's imagination. Many whales are sighted again and again, but there are always new ones showing up. A temporary name or number is assigned until the whale is formally christened at the annual spring gathering of humpback-whale researchers. It is hosted by a leading whale-research group, the Center for Coastal Studies, in Provincetown, Massachusetts. Most of the east-coast American and Canadian researchers attend, and toast each new whale as they vote before each christening.

About 3,000 humpbacks, a quarter of the estimated world population, convene at Silver Bank, in the Caribbean, every January after a month-long

A humpback whale waves its tail flukes. Each tail's underside has a distinct black-and-white pattern, ranging from nearly all black to nearly all white. These fluke patterns enable researchers to identify humpbacks individually.

PHOTOGRAPH: JANE GIBBS

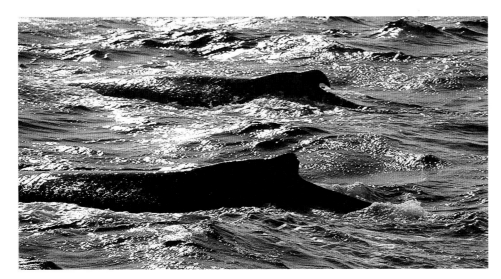

Humpback whales break the surface. The humpback's small dorsal fin, sometimes only a nub, sits on a platform or hump that rises up from the back.

PHOTOGRAPH: WILLIAM ROSSITER

southerly swim. It is an unlikely family reunion—thousands of decidedly reptilian sea mammals each as big as a boxcar. Some are singers, some fighters, some mothers and calves with or without escorts—all going about their business. Beneath the cover of the waves and the wind, below the surface of the sea, there is a steady humming punctuated by cries, brays, and whistles. It is a special world, a world of sound.

Comet is a 46-foot-long mature male. As he puts his head down and hangs motionless about 100 feet below the surface in the classic singer's pose, he forces sound through the air passages in his head. First, he makes a series of low rumbles, then, squeezing tighter, he issues trumpetlike high passages. This is the song Comet has heard over and over again, the same song that he and every other male sing. For 10 or 11 minutes, he blows about six themes, then repeats them in the same sequence. At some point during one of the themes, he surfaces for air and takes three quick breaths. But he does not stop singing. The singers, only the males, can go on for half an hour or for an entire morning. Some whales sing night and day.

Researchers call these vocalizations "song," because they have a formal structure; there are also some musical elements. Knowing many humpbacks as individuals, researchers attribute some poetry to the systematic arrangement of growls, creaks, honks, and other odd noises—though, in some ways, male humpbacks sound more like braying steers than singing poets. Music or not, male humpbacks make these sounds for several months every winter, and the song changes gradually through the season and from year to year. Still, at any given time, all the male humpbacks singing in the North Atlantic are singing essentially the same song.

Only Comet and his fellow humpbacks know precisely why humpbacks sing, and on this matter, they are silent. But a marine zoologist with some imagination looks to other animals' behavior for a plausible theory. Jim Darling, who has studied humpback whales off Hawaii and British Columbia, looks to mountain goats and sheep. "It's all a matter of horns," he says. "Male ungulates compare horns, and the one with the biggest set gets access to the female. It's only when the 'racks' are about the same size that males need to fight." Such subtle visual clues, of course, cannot be read underwater. Darling thinks that male humpbacks may use sound because it travels well underwater: "Perhaps the one who sings best has the best chance for mating. And if matters can't be decided on the basis of the songs, they fight it out." These groups of fighting whales—called "surface active groups"—are made up of males of all ages, as well as the odd female.

After a morning of singing, Comet is eager to test his mettle. As a full-grown male, he is a candidate for mating privileges this year. He races toward several males in a surface active group and blows a curtain of bubbles out his blowholes. The challenge! Torch, a smaller, young male, moves away and turns his tail toward Comet. Sensing the possibility of taking advantage, Comet charges, seeking to land a decisive blow. In the final seconds of the charge, he turns his reptilian snout as if to throw a shoulder block, and rolls into the younger male. Torch, however, is waiting. With the quickness of youth, he lifts his tail. The barnacles attached to the edges of his flukes are glistening, sharp—the most powerful weapon of this mammalian boxcar. Smash! Comet's back recoils from the blow. The barnacles have dug into his cartilaginous dorsal fin, and blood oozes, dripping along his back. But the blood coagulates in the salt water. It is only a superficial wound. Torch raises his tail clear out of the water to strike again. He is dripping some blood, too. Then Comet rams him from the side. Torch has had enough. He moves a safe few yards away and watches six or seven males charge around at the surface, blowing threatening bubble streams underwater. All talk, no action. Comet's bluster appears to have made them wary. He has won the challenge.

The sounds of singing, fighting males travel far and wide across Silver Bank. Several miles away, Talon, only six years old, is nurturing her first calf, Rush, born in January. Talon hears the male songs but is not interested in mating. She is nursing, devoted. Later that day, however, she lets Comet travel with them as an escort. Suddenly, Comet becomes a patient male, waiting to mate and willing to let Talon say when.

A humpback whale executes a tail breach on the mating grounds off the British Virgin Islands in the Caribbean. A tail breach can be part of play or battle. Male humpbacks, fighting over access to females in heat, use their powerful tails to lash other males.

PHOTOGRAPH: DAVID MATTILA,
COURTESY HARRIET CORBETT

Also off from the big groups is Beltane. She gave birth to a calf, Cat Eyes, two years earlier, and she travels alone, biding her time. Perhaps she will mate next year and become a mother again.

Of all the named humpbacks, the females Beltane and Talon are two of the most loved by North Atlantic whale researchers. Phil Clapham, of the Center for Coastal Studies, pinned his study of humpback reproductive behavior on them. Beltane is the 1980 calf of Silver. (First sighted in 1979, Silver had lost half a fluke, probably to a ship propeller.) Talon is the 1981 calf of Sinestra. When Beltane had Cat Eyes in 1985 and Talon had Rush in 1987, they gave their mothers the first documented humpback grandchildren. They proved to Clapham and the scientific world that humpbacks attain sexual maturity as early as age four or five. Thereafter, they reproduce every one to three years.

Both Beltane and Talon won the hearts of researchers and whale watchers with their eagerness to play and perform around boats. Throughout the summer of 1985, when Beltane and her son, Cat Eyes, appeared, they were, according to Clapham, "the two most outrageous and curious whales of the season." After 31 sightings, Cat Eyes was voted "calf of the year." Talon herself was calf of the year, in 1981, and inspired the same sort of fierce researcher loyalty. Now, with her first calf, Rush, her appeal has doubled.

Whale watching is fun for researchers, and it provides an opportunity to do some science, but what do the whales get out of it besides momentary distraction?

The decade-long association—call it a collaboration—between scientist and humpback whale has already yielded important conservation rewards. In October 1986, as a result of the efforts of the Center for Coastal Studies and several conservation groups—not to mention the basic appeal of the whales—Joaquin Balagaer, president of the Dominican Republic, set aside Silver Bank as a whale sanctuary, the first in the North Atlantic. This crucial act protects the warm-water habitat, the winter vacation home, of the humpbacks. Every winter, the males sing and fight; the females bestow access to their charms and give birth to more calves. Life is to be lived.

The humpback whale Talon, while still a youngster, exposes her "claw" for all to see. In 1981, she was voted calf of the year.
PHOTOGRAPH: CENTER
FOR COASTAL STUDIES

IN THE SAME WARM CARIBBEAN WATERS, THERE ARE TINY free-floating larvae of barnacles searching for a place to call home and on which to travel north. Barnacles belong to the group of animals called crustaceans, which includes shrimp, lobsters, and crabs. Writing more than a century ago, Harvard naturalist Louis Agassiz described the barnacle as "nothing more than a little shrimplike animal, standing on its head in a limestone house and kicking food into its mouth." Although most of the world's 800 species of barnacles are content to live out their days on a single rock, several species, particularly acorn barnacles, prefer what may be best described as sedentary life in the fast lane.

To a barnacle, the humpback whale Comet, surfacing periodically, is like a rock in the intertidal zone. But there is one important difference: Comet is moving. He will take the barnacle to food-rich areas and, perhaps more important, will keep it safe from starfish and other predators. Humpbacks and

A humpback-whale mother and calf drift
through the warm waters of a tropical sea.
Calves are born in winter in the tropics.
They remain close to their mothers for
most of the first year and sometimes into
the second.

PHOTOGRAPH: FLIP NICKLIN

Spinner dolphins swim in the clear winter waters of the tropical Atlantic. Spinners are common to all tropical seas. Feeding on fish and squid, they sometimes follow the warm eddies of the Gulf Stream as it moves north in spring.

PHOTOGRAPH: RUSSELL WID COFFIN

Barnacles grow on the chin of a humpback whale. The same species of barnacles found on rocks thrive on slower-moving whales. The round scars on the humpback show evidence of barnacles that have been scraped off or otherwise dislodged—perhaps during a fight.

PHOTOGRAPH: CENTER FOR
COASTAL STUDIES

Among the more common barnacles that live on humpbacks are acorn barnacles. Barnacles prefer the lips, chin, throat, flippers, flukes, and belly, particularly the area around the sex organs. Once attached, they suck part of the whale's skin into the outer cavity of their shell, forming an adhesive seal.

PHOTOGRAPH: SCOTT KRAUS,
NEW ENGLAND AQUARIUM

other barnacle-encrusted whales move slowly at times, but not so slowly that a starfish can crawl over them and seize a few barnacles. The relationship between Comet and the barnacles, though rather one sided, is not especially harmful to the humpback. It can, however, turn affection, parental or conjugal, between humpbacks into a delicate, awkward business. One territory the barnacles favor is on the belly around the sex organs. Making love, perhaps even nursing, can be painful. Fortunately, the whales' thick skin protects them during close-up encounters. And maybe the barnacles keep all but the most passionate and fit males from mating. That could have survival value for the species.

A young barnacle, as free-floating larvae and part of the ocean's minute planktonic world, finds a humpback host mainly through luck. In their travels, fish eat most of the larvae as part of their plankton diet. But during a crucial two-to four-week period, some lucky larvae catch a humpback like Comet napping, or swimming slowly, and when they do, they hop aboard. The larvae may also be attracted by a strong chemical extract that their hermaphroditic parents seem to leave on the humpback. When receptors in the larvae's antennae recognize this attractive substance, the successful young barnacles attach themselves, through antennules, to Comet's back. Growing quickly, the barnacles suck part of Comet's skin into the outer cavity of their shell. In time, the whale's skin grows around and over the sides of the shell, forming an adhesive seal.

The barnacles compete for the best spots: Comet's lips, chin, throat, flippers, flukes, and belly. Some barnacles even grow on top of others. Once established, they settle in. Growing fast now, they are getting ready for the roller-coaster ride of their lives. The barnacles on Talon and her calf, Rush, will be travelling north first: female humpbacks, recent mothers, generally feel the urge to eat a little sooner than most males. Talon and Rush may abandon their escort, Comet, and if Torch or another male wants to join them, he will have to keep his distance—the female's choice. The winter groupings of singers, surface active groups, and mothers and calves with or without escorts tend to break down on migration and on the northern feeding grounds. The exception is mothers and calves—they are inseparable. The migration starts in March, and by April, all the singers will have left. For eight or nine months, the Caribbean will be quiet.

IN THE COOLER, CALM INSHORE WATERS OFF GEORGIA, ABOUT 1,000 miles northwest of the humpback whales' winter retreat, Stripe, a 40-foot-long, 40-ton right whale, swims back and forth in the shallows as her labor pains come on. It is early January. She has carried this growing life inside her for about a year. She is alone, but she has been through this before. At least 30 years old, according to researchers, she is an experienced mother. Nonetheless, labor, common to all mammalian mothers, comes in waves of sharp, intense contractions and is all-demanding. The baby always seems too large. After hours of pain, Stripe pushes her smooth-skinned newborn into the water in an explosion of bubbles. A female, the baby is 14 feet long and weighs about a ton. She is almost slender, unlike her bulky mother. At first, she appears lifeless. Stripe nudges her. Stripe is exhausted, but she manages to push her to the surface. The air is the smack of reality as the calf takes her first breath through the pair of blowholes at the top of her head. For the rest of her life, this calf, like all whales and dolphins, will be tethered to the surface, forced to return every few minutes to breathe.

For several days, Stripe and her calf rest some 300 yards off the beach. They stay at or close to the surface. The nearest other mother and calf are a mile or more away. Stripe and her calf stay side by side, completely involved in each other. They do little except nurse and rest, rest and nurse. In 9 or 10 weeks, they will depart on the long migration, the mother's hunger urging

A right-whale mother and calf rest off northern Florida on February 15, 1987. A newborn right is usually about 14 feet long and weighs about a ton. A calf stays close to its mother in shallow, inshore waters.

PHOTOGRAPH: MOIRA BROWN,

NEW ENGLAND AQUARIUM

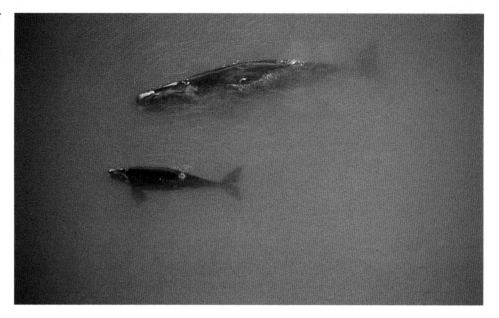

them north to the cold waters, where, in late spring, abundant plankton bloom. For now, however, the cool sea off Georgia and northern Florida is ideal for the calf's "bath water." The temperature is neither too warm nor too cold, allowing mother and calf to conserve their energy.

It is a tender scene, this giant mother and her oversize calf resting and nursing. It is a quiet scene, except for the occasional hum of Poseidon nuclear submarines sailing in and out of Kings Bay, Georgia.

In the last decade, at least five North Atlantic right whales have died in ship collisions, their tails sometimes severed by propellers. Five percent of the known living rights bear ship-strike marks. All whale species are accidentally injured or killed by ships at times, but right whales seem to be the most vulnerable. Most of their activities—feeding, playing, courting—occur at or near the surface and close to shore, and they are slower than most whales. Near Kings Bay, a favorite calving area, there is concern that a mother and calf could be so absorbed in nursing and resting that they may not notice approaching or surfacing submarines. The submarines are more than 400 feet long and not very maneuverable on the surface. Soon the 500-foot-long Trident submarines will arrive, and there will be extensive dredging to deepen the channel. The new traffic will increase the likelihood of collision between ships or submarines and rights.

Or the right whales may run into one of the U.S. Navy's "fighter dolphins." The navy is training bottlenose dolphins to patrol the harbor. In the wild, bottlenose dolphins are friendly and travel peaceably through these waters alongside right whales. Trained for mayhem, however, fighter dolphins may even ram rights wandering too close to a submarine. They may not be able to hurt the bulky rights, but they could certainly harass them.

Probably no whale has suffered more at the hands of humans than the right whale. Certainly, no whale comes closer today to courting biological oblivion. As a result of whaling, humpbacks were reduced from an estimated

A right-whale mother nuzzles her calf. The white patches on their heads are callosities—raised patches of roughened skin—found only on rights. The patches are covered in cyamids, or whale lice.

PHOTOGRAPH: GREGORY STONE,
NEW ENGLAND AQUARIUM

world population of more than 125,000 to about 12,000 today. But rights, whose total population was once estimated at 50,000, now number as few as 3,000. Most of these are southern right whales. They look like northern right whales but are geographically separate and are considered a different species. In the North Atlantic, only about 300 to 350 rights are left.

Dubbed *Eubalaena glacialis* by scientists, the northern right obtained its common name during the whaling era. To hunters, this whale was the "right" one to kill, as it was not too difficult to catch and provided lots of product for relatively little effort. The right whale is massive in girth, about 60 percent of its length, and often floated when harpooned. A large right yielded 80 barrels of oil and 1,000 pounds of baleen. Beginning in the eleventh century, Basque, English, and Dutch whalers killed thousands of them off Europe using hand-held harpoons. By 1530, rights were becoming so scarce off Europe that Basque whalers sailed from Britain to Iceland, then to Newfoundland and Labrador, hunting local populations along the way. Early settlers to the east coast of Canada and the United States needed ready sources of oil for their lamps and to make soap. By the late eighteenth century, few right whales had survived. Later, the demand for women's accessories such as lipstick (made from oil from the whale's blubber) and corsets and umbrellas (made from the whale's long, flexible baleen plates) helped keep the population to a few stragglers. By the early 1900s, there were perhaps only a few dozen in the North Atlantic.

Whale research featuring photo-identification studies of humpback whales began around North America in the 1970s. At that time, few experts thought that there were enough right whales left to maintain the species, much less to mount a study in the North Atlantic. Those few who did want to study them went to the wild Patagonian coast of Argentina and concentrated on southern rights. But in 1980, on an aerial survey of the Bay of Fundy, researchers counted 19 northern rights in one day. Interest in working with them gained momentum.

ON JANUARY 7, SCOTT KRAUS, A RESEARCHER AT THE NEW England Aquarium, in Boston, Massachusetts, flies low along the northern Florida coast near Jacksonville. He sees Stripe and her new calf, and he becomes excited. Kraus, his associate Amy Knowlton, and others have been monitoring right whales off Florida and Georgia since he discovered the calving grounds here in 1985. He tells the pilot of the two-seater Cessna 152 to turn for another pass. Kraus wants to photograph Stripe and her calf, "to get their IDs." This is one of the earliest sightings of the year. The calf is the fifth one known born to Stripe, one of the more frequently sighted rights and among the first to be identified.

Stripe was "stripeless" when first photographed off the Florida coast in February 1967. She got her name later from the broad scar on her nose—a wound from an encounter with a boat or from banging into the ocean bottom in late 1980 or early 1981. She had a calf with her in 1967 and again in 1974. In 1981, soon after the New England Aquarium research program got under way, Stripe posed with a third calf, Stars, who has grown up with the research program. Stripe is doing her part to reverse right-whale extinction. Her progeny are helping, too. At age five, in 1986, Stars had her first calf and became the youngest documented right-whale mother.

Even without her scar, Stripe can be identified, and so can Stars. The secret of right-whale identification lies in the callosity patterns, the distinctive marks on every right's head. Callosities, resembling calluses, are raised patches of roughened skin that form on all right whales in about the same spots that humans acquire facial hair: on top of the head, around the lips, and on the chin. Researcher Roger Payne, who is based in Massachusetts and has a field station in Argentina to study South Atlantic rights, devised the callosity-pattern identity system with several associates. The callosity patterns are subtler than the tail patterns used to identify humpbacks, but they work if one has a sharp photograph. Photographing rights off New England since 1981, aquarium researchers—together with researchers from the Center for Coastal Studies, the University of Rhode Island, and the Woods Hole Oceanographic Institution—have identified 288 right whales in the North Atlantic, mostly from their callosities.

Callosities are gray but appear white against the black skin of the whale. A closer look shows that the "whiteness" is sometimes yellow, orange, or pink. The shades of color come from cyamids, or whale lice, that live on rights as barnacles do on humpbacks.

Barnacles and cyamids are both crustaceans. But while barnacles anchor themselves on the whale, cyamids move around. Right-whale callosities are literally crawling with whale lice, though the lice do not go far.

There are 22 known species of whale lice (*Cyamus*), all unrelated to the lice that afflict humans. Whale lice are less than an inch long and look like variations on the theme of a tiny crab. They are found on most species of baleen whales, particularly humpback and gray whales, and a few of the toothed whales. Most whale-lice species have their favorite hosts, but some are not choosy and will go for any one of several whale species.

Five different *Cyamus* species live on right whales. The typical cyamid holds on to its whale host with 10 strong legs, each with a sharply curved hook at the end. A cyamid born on Stripe must grab hold as soon as it emerges, weak-legged, from its mother's marsupium, or pouch. It will mature, mate, and molt, always keeping hold with at least a few of its legs. It will live its seafaring life, from birth to death, on Stripe, holding on tight as Stripe breaches, lobs her tail, nudges and bumps against her calf, and plows through the water. This is why the cyamid tends to choose areas on the whale

Three *Cyamus* species move around on a right whale. Cyamids are crustaceans, each less than an inch long. In 1985, this right whale was killed by a ship near Provincetown, Massachusetts.
PHOTOGRAPH: SCOTT KRAUS,
NEW ENGLAND AQUARIUM

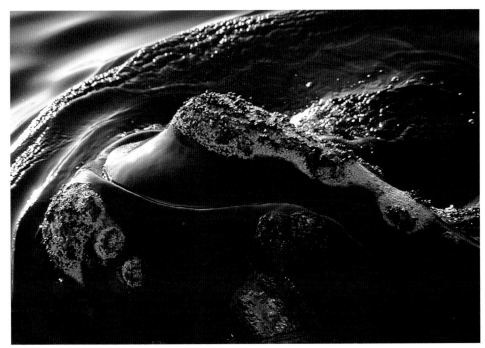

A right-whale calf surfaces, showing its "bonnet," the name whalers gave to the callosities at the top of the head. As the whale matures, the shape and pattern of the callosities become fairly constant and useful for identification.
PHOTOGRAPH: SCOTT KRAUS,
NEW ENGLAND AQUARIUM

that have reduced water flow, such as callosities. A cyamid needs to have a good grip. One slip, and it is burial at sea. Whale lice spend much of their lives underwater on whales, but they cannot swim.

Researcher Victoria Rowntree, who works with Roger Payne in his Massachusetts laboratory, once cultured cyamids at the New England Aquarium for several months to find out what they eat and whether they are parasites or just passengers. She saw them holding their mouth parts flat against a piece of whale skin and moving secondary antennae-like projections on either side of the mouth. She could not prove that they were eating the skin but found that their intestines became dark, presumably from the top layers of skin, which contain pigment. Later, she found more evidence of eating skin: cyamids taken from a humpback's white skin on its tail had white intestines, while cyamids taken from black skin had black intestines. Do cyamids harm their whale prey? "Whales continually slough their skin," writes Rowntree. "And cyamids may simply take advantage of this." Even though some of the skin is living tissue, such a food source is unlikely to be consumed. Whales are *big*.

In one way, whale lice are beneficial. Without the brightly colored cyamids, researchers would find it harder to see the callosity patterns used to identify right whales. In the early months of life, a calf is so covered in cyamids that its callosity pattern is a blur, and researchers must wait. After the calf reaches age six months, however, the callosities with cyamids stay fairly constant. Individual identification of rights enables researchers to determine abundance, longevity, birth and death rate, movement, and social behavior. For right whales more than any other whale species, their precarious future depends on researchers keeping track of them.

THROUGHOUT JANUARY AND FEBRUARY, STRIPE NURSES HER calf. High-fat milk is dispensed in jets from two teats located in slits just above the genitals on her glossy white belly. The calf suckles persistently, gaining perhaps a ton or more a month. The calf needs as much weight as she can gain for the long migration ahead.

Meanwhile, other rights, like humpbacks, scuffle in surface active groups, and some of them end up mating. Unlike the humpbacks, however, the rights will continue their amorous escapades throughout the year—even on the feeding grounds up north. There is another difference: the rights, with their low moans and assorted belches, are noisy, but they do not sing.

One evening in early March, a storm at sea, far to the east, brings long, rolling swells. By midnight, the wind and the waves off northern Florida come up together. The sudden severity of the blow is unusual for this late in the day. For protection, Stripe takes her calf five miles out from shore. In the night, drifting out at sea, she notices that the water is warmer than it has been in some time. Spring is coming! Time to head north! Before morning, Stripe and her calf move to the outer edge of the continental shelf and into the intense blue of the Gulf Stream. Hunger. Food. Migration.

The Gulf Stream cuts a wide swath through the North Atlantic. Equal to the volume of all the world's rivers times five, it is one of the ocean's fastest currents, moving at surface speeds of up to five knots, more than eight

Atlantic spotted dolphins travel in groups of 20 to 50 or sometimes more than 100. Feeding on fish and squid, they prefer the warm waters of the North Atlantic. Along with bottlenose and striped dolphins, they sometimes meet humpback and right whales on migration and travel with them for miles.

PHOTOGRAPH: INTERNATIONAL FUND FOR ANIMAL WELFARE

feet per second. Stripe and her calf—rights are slow swimmers as whales go—are happy to have help. The humpbacks, though speedier and more agile, also ride the current. Swimming steadily north for about 10 days now, the humpbacks Beltane, Talon, and Rush are followed at a distance by Comet and a few others. They travel far out at sea on a vector that will pass Bermuda and intersect with the migration route of the rights somewhere off North Carolina. It will take a month of steady swimming for each species to reach the feeding grounds off New England and eastern Canada. Meanwhile, just for fun, visiting dolphins—spotted, striped, and bottlenose—swim circles around the lumbering, migrating whales.

Some humpbacks use the Bermuda area for three to four weeks in April. Midway between their winter Caribbean breeding grounds and their summer North Atlantic feeding grounds, they stop to eat. Before the whaling era, they may have also used Bermuda waters for breeding. American researchers Greg Stone and Steve Katona and Bermudan Edward Tucker suggest that if humpbacks return to their former numbers, Bermuda may well be repopulated during the winter. But for now, it is only a pit stop: Beltane, Talon, Rush, and Comet are eager to push on.

The humpbacks turn west-northwest, toward the continent. They move steadily, and by the Carolinas, they are a few miles from the migration track of the rights. The two species are rapidly converging. The North Carolina rendezvous, occurring off Cape Hatteras, where the Gulf Stream turns sharply out to sea, is a migration scene comparable in scale to the wildlife parades on the great Serengeti Plain of Africa. Instead of wildebeests, giraffes, and gazelles, the Cape Hatteras scene features big, slow, bulky rights and leathery, comparatively lithe humpbacks, both spread out over a wide area. Numerous bottlenose dolphins stay with them, sometimes for miles. The dolphins, jumping, sliding along the surface, often chase schooling fishes such as menhaden, eating them en route. By the time the migration reaches northern

Sperm whales swim in a mixed nursery school consisting of mothers, juveniles, and calves. Mature males travel separately. They grow up to 60 feet in length; females, up to only 40 feet. At birth, calves are 11 to 14 feet long and weigh about a ton. The sperm's huge square head, one-quarter to one-third or more of its body length, has a large reservoir of a white, waxy substance called "spermaceti," long sought by whalers to make a high-quality oil.

Once a day, between bouts of deep diving and feeding, sperm whales come together to socialize. They like to touch each other and exchange sounds, patterns of clicks called "codas." Shy animals, sperms are more approachable in these tight groups.

PHOTOGRAPHS: INTERNATIONAL FUND FOR ANIMAL WELFARE

A young right whale stares at another species, a look of curiosity that seems to pass for recognition.

PHOTOGRAPH: FLIP NICKLIN

New Jersey, most of the bottlenose dolphins will be gone, having turned south and followed schools of fish inshore.

Day by day, Beltane, Talon, Rush, Comet, and the other humpbacks, along with Stripe, her calf, and several other rights, keep moving. Sensitive to the currents and the temperatures, they return to their separate ocean paths. The humpbacks pass leatherback and loggerhead turtles. One afternoon, spinner dolphins, warm-water lovers, approach the migrators and give a freeform show, performing their spinning leaps almost in the humpbacks' path. The next morning, the humpbacks meet a group of sperm whales, a "mixed nursery school" with mothers and calves ranging in length from 20 to 35 feet. The toothed whales hang just beneath the surface, tawny logs rolling in the swells, as if inviting an interspecies encounter.

Comet fixes his eye on a female sperm whale. It is a look across the species barrier—two non-threatening species plainly curious about the other. The baleen whale meets the toothed whale close up. Two of the most highly evolved whales, profoundly divided by their eating habits, look at each other across tens of millions of years of separate evolution.

But the sperms, extremely shy, back off. They send out slow click trains that sound like loose change banging away in an empty dryer. Comet, the reptilian singer, rarely sings on migration or around strangers. He can issue only a low growl and hang there, staring at the wrinkled, angular, brownish sperms. Finally, the sperms depart. Most of the females dive deep, down to the canyons just off the continental shelf to hunt for giant squid. But a few mothers stay near the surface to tend their calves.

Almost anything can be seen in the great Gulf Stream. This year, it runs close to shore, pushed in part by odd northeast winds. There are warm-water sharks darting about everywhere, but days later, they give way to the cooler-water varieties. The humpback whales, crossing out of the main part of the Gulf Stream, move from an intensely blue world into one that seems closer to dark green. They luxuriate in the cooler water, feeling it stream off their faces and along their fins like a cool wind on the final stretch of a marathon. They notice the plankton becoming more numerous. The fish and krill and other organisms will grow fat on these plankton. Soon there will be food for all.

Sperm whales, mainly in search of squid, dive deep off the continental shelf to 3,000 feet and, in some cases, almost two miles. They range throughout the world ocean, though usually stay far from shore, on the high seas, for easy access to their canyon hunting grounds.

PHOTOGRAPH: INTERNATIONAL FUND FOR ANIMAL WELFARE

IT IS ON THIS COMPLEX
*pyramid of life—one species depending on another*
*on another on another—that whales,*
*the largest creatures of all, rely.*

# SPRING

**T**HE GULF STREAM, tracing its broad path toward Britain, floods the surface of the North Atlantic Ocean with warm water. In the tropics and the warm temperate zone, it flows over cold intermediate and deep waters. Chiefly because of the temperature difference, there is a barrier, or thermocline. The waters do not mix. But in the cooler temperate and Arctic waters, the Gulf Stream dissipates and turns cooler. Little of its warmth ever reaches eastern Canada and the northeastern United States. The offshore surface waters there, except in the hottest part of summer, stay almost as cold as the waters at the bottom, allowing them to mix. In some northern areas, powerful underwater currents pour over underwater mountain passes and flood wide, rocky valleys. When the deep waters hit steep, rising underwater trenches, they surge to the surface. This "upwelling" is the secret to the fertility of the northern North Atlantic and is the reason why whales like it as a feeding ground; in tropical waters, on the other hand, the lack of upwelling explains why there is much less food there. Upwelling has created some of the great fishing areas of the world, such as the Grand Banks of Newfoundland.

Upwelling brings to the sunny upper sea layers the nutrients nitrogen and phosphorus, which largely come from the fecal matter and the dead bodies of millions of tiny sea animals. These nutrients are needed for the growth of drifting marine plants known as phytoplankton. The nutrients are useless unless driven up into the water column, because most plants need the light that permeates the top 300-foot layer of the sea. Photosynthesis, which literally means "putting together with light," is essential to plant growth.

These drifting sea plants grow according to the phases of the moon. Some reproduce only during a full moon; other plankton reach their peak in abundance at that time. This growth is caused partly by the moon's influence on the tides and partly by the varying intensity of polarized light. When conditions are right, though many of these plants are microscopic, they can be extraordinarily profuse. A single milligram of phosphoric oxide, one of the two essential nutrients for plant plankton, enables an estimated 9 million diatoms to flourish.

Diatoms are one-celled or colonial algae, and they may be the most important single foodstuff in the sea. These tiny "lower" plants, able to photosynthesize, are made of living tissue encased in a hard silica shell. For the most part, they drift at sea, but sometimes they collect on whales. Blue whales, for example, were called "sulphur-bottoms" by whalers, who noticed that massive colonies of diatoms made the whales' bellies appear yellowish. Copepods—the favorite food of right whales—love to eat diatoms. These small crustaceans can devour their weight in diatoms in one day. Even mussels and oysters eat diatoms. Diatoms and other phytoplankton provide food for zooplankton, which include the young and tiny animals of many species that, in turn, provide food for fish, young squid, certain other crustaceans, and whales.

All of this occurs in the top 300-foot layer of the sea. These plants, along with the majority of these animals, spend most of their lives in this layer. It is a thin skin over an ocean that is up to 600 feet deep in the Great South Channel, about 60 miles southeast of Cape Cod. And in some parts, the ocean drops to more than six miles; the average depth is two miles.

It is on this complex pyramid of life—each species depending on another on another on another—that whales, the largest creatures of all, rely. When something goes wrong, the chain breaks and the whole pyramid may crash, as it does from time to time in certain areas. Whales, able travellers, usually move on, but they are sometimes driven to less-productive feeding areas. Sometimes they must chase prey that are less tasty and less nutritious and that may carry contaminants.

Page 25:
Gannets flock to Cape St. Mary's, on the southwest coast of Newfoundland's Avalon Peninsula.

PHOTOGRAPH: DOTTE LARSEN

IN THE EARLY-MORNING HOURS OF APRIL 20, A SLUDGE BARGE steams out of New York City to the 106-mile dump site, precisely 106 miles east of Cape May, New Jersey. A month earlier, the barge had to travel only 12 miles, to the New York Bight, to do its dumping. But the bight became so polluted—with the effects felt as far away as the pretty beaches of Long Island—that the dump had to be moved farther out to sea. More than a third of the waste comes from New York City. It is mostly sewage sludge, the solid matter left after sewage waste is treated. But some of it is toxic sludge, most of which comes from northern New Jersey's chemical and industrial manufacturing belt, and it contains toxic metals such as cadmium and lead. Some 328,200 dry tons of sludge are being dumped in this area each year. Recent federal and state laws make dumping at sea illegal after 1991. Yet New York City claims that it cannot meet that timetable until the late 1990s. Meanwhile, the dumping continues.

In the rolling sea, the captain and the crew of the sludge barge are intent on their job and do not see Comet, Beltane, and the other migrating humpback whales. The whales take little notice of the barge. The waste is dumped overboard, and in a few minutes, it is neatly covered by water. But it is not gone. Little is lost in the world ocean. Most things are only diluted, carried elsewhere, and eventually cycled throughout the system.

Another source of pollution is the Earth's atmosphere. The story of radioactive tritium from nuclear-bomb testing in the upper atmosphere reveals what can happen. After the explosions, which occurred in the late 1950s and the early 1960s—until the atmospheric test-ban treaty of 1963—the tritium fell to earth over Siberia and Alaska in rain and snow. From there, it entered various rivers that flow into the Arctic, and was carried into the deep ocean off Labrador and Greenland. This tritium-tagged water is now somewhere off Bermuda, creeping along the bottom in a giant tongue. It is not a matter for environmental concern, because it has decayed to low levels. Yet it shows how a contaminant can move through the larger atmo-

After the long migration, a humpback-whale mother and her calf arrive on the northern feeding grounds in the Gulf of Maine.

PHOTOGRAPH: DOTTE LARSEN

sphere-ocean system, from several miles in the air to the deep ocean across the Arctic, in just 30 years.

Deep-ocean sludge dumping, oil spills, and persistent run-offs of oil and pesticides into rivers and eventually into the sea are already having far-reaching effects. Every year, thousands of shore birds are caught in oil slicks. The shells of their eggs are thinned by pesticides, mostly DDT, banned in the U.S. and Canada long ago but still lingering in the environment. Many spawning beds for fish and other marine life have been ruined. The fish and the shellfish found in the harbors of North America are simply unfit for human consumption. An underwater visit to the 12-mile dump site in the New York Bight reveals a horror-movie scene: fish eggs and larvae with cancerous growths, crabs with black, fouled gills. The only thriving resident on the bottom is the *capitella* worm, a species known for its fondness for sludge whether it contains polychlorinated biphenyls (PCBs), heavy metals, or viral and bacterial pathogens. The New York Bight has it all. The new 106-mile site, if used for dumping for a few more years, will be the same.

Passing the sludge dump, the humpbacks refuse to be put off their food. Swimming alongside Long Island, they feel the water turn colder. As they

Humpback whales feed in the Gulf of Maine. Each, in turn, swims to the surface, collecting fish and water. Mouth open, the whale lets the water spill out over the sides of the lower jaw. Humpbacks prefer schooling fishes such as sand lance. They also feed on krill.

PHOTOGRAPH: WILLIAM ROSSITER

round Cape Cod, the shores and the bottom topography change from sand to mostly rock. The whales roll into Massachusetts Bay, at the southern end of the Gulf of Maine, and Beltane, Talon, and Rush, followed by Comet, spread out. First, they investigate popular Stellwagen Bank, an 18-mile-long underwater glacial deposit of sand and gravel that is north of Cape Cod. Shallow and sandy compared with the sea floor around it, Stellwagen Bank ranges from 60 to more than 125 feet deep. The eight-inch-long sand lance, one of the humpbacks' favorite fishes, lives here, though last year the population crashed on the bank due to the downturn of an apparently natural population cycle. The humpbacks had to dine elsewhere. This year, the humpbacks find that the sand-lance population is recovering slowly.

Comet sees a sand-lance school wriggling through the water like eels. As he noses close, they turn and race for the bottom. They bury themselves in the sand. Comet notices that there are plenty of copepods for the sand lance to eat. Yet there are still not enough sand lance to guarantee steady feeding for a hungry humpback. Comet heads back out to sea, east, then southeast, toward Georges Bank. At Great South Channel, he finds some dense schools of sand lance and hundreds of other feeding humpback whales, along with some minke and fin whales. On the wing and diving for the same food are red-necked phalaropes, sooty and greater shearwaters, and common terns. And dozens of herring gulls.

Comet dives straight down, driving fast with his wide tail into the clear, cold water, which almost stings his lips. Then he swivels around. Using his long flippers, he turns upright and ascends in the water column. When he is 40 or 50 feet from the surface, he opens his mouth and the water rushes in, along with his dinner. His accordion-like throat grooves expand. Several barnacles that had settled in the grooves fall off, victims of the abrupt expansion of their habitat. As Comet breaks the surface, mouth first, he closes his jaws. Some of the water spills out over his lips; the rest streams out between his baleen plates. The water gone, he swallows his reward: a few bite-sized sand lance.

Humpback whales, like right, fin, minke, and blue whales, have baleen plates instead of teeth. They cannot chew but swallow their food whole. Baleen grows from the roof of the whale's mouth in rows of plates that suggest the slats of a Venetian blind. Each flexible slat has a fringe of stiff bristles on the inside that help hold in the fish or krill while the water flows out between the slats. Depending on the species of whale, baleen comes in various lengths, widths, and colors, including white, yellow, gray, and black. Humpback whales have between 300 and 400 plates on each side of the upper jaw, each plate ranging from about 2 to 2-1/2 feet in length. Minke whales, the smallest of the baleen whales at up to only about 35 feet long, have the shortest baleen, as small as a foot. Right whales have the longest, up to 8 feet. Their long baleen allows them to strain a larger mouthful of the smaller organisms they prefer. Also, rights must have bigger mouths to start with: they have no throat grooves, and their mouths cannot expand.

Humpbacks and other baleen whales are sometimes called "ocean grazers," in contrast to the toothy fish- and squid-eating pilot whales, harbor porpoises, and various dolphins. But humpbacks are not "cows of the sea" *or*

Hungry gulls swoop down to pick out sand lance from a humpback whale's mouth seconds before it closes. A humpback can eat up to two tons of food a day, or 2 to 4 percent of its body weight.

PHOTOGRAPH: JANE GIBBS

gentle herbivores. They are predators who use their considerable wits to catch fish and krill that are constantly on the move.

In Great South Channel, the sand lance are not so tightly schooled as a humpback would like them to be. Comet decides to blow a "bubble net." From 60 feet down, he sights the scattered sand lance and blows bubbles in a wide circle to surround them. As the bubble net rises, confining and concentrating the fish, Comet dives deep and comes up through the bubbles, mouth wide open. As he gulps the water, his throat expands to form a giant pouch, increasing the potential volume of a mouthful. Breaking the surface, he closes his jaws and uses his tongue to squeeze out the water between his baleen plates. This time, there are more fish, plus a few tasty shrimplike krill, or euphausiids. Comet tries again and soon finds that he has started something. All around him, other humpbacks are blowing bubbles, then coming up inside bubble nets. In an area the size of a football field, there are 10 bubble nets in a row. Then it is Talon's turn. She blows a bubble net while Rush, her calf, watches.

The herring gulls love the bubble nets, too. Diving into the water, they scoop a few sand lance or krill seconds before the open-mouthed whales emerge. The gulls even take a few herring from the whales' mouths. Comet nearly catches a bird when he snaps his jaw shut.

After an afternoon of feeding, the humpbacks leap high out of the water in joyful celebration. The gulls cry overhead, and the springtime sun blinks on the rolling sea. The humpbacks feel good to be full after the long oceanic journey. They should have six to eight months of good meals now, with plenty of time off for playing and for watching the boatloads of whale watchers who will soon be coming to see them.

Also welcoming the chance to feed are Comet's shipmates—the barnacles that survived the journey north and the rambunctious arrival of the humpbacks' feeding season. When Comet submerges, each barnacle opens its shell and waves its whiplike plume through the water, drawing the plankton-laden current toward its mouth. As Comet breaks the water in a feeding lunge or a leap, each barnacle closes—except for a small breathing hole between the valves of its shell.

The acorn barnacles on Comet and other humpbacks have travelled several thousand miles. In the cold northern plankton-rich waters, Comet's barnacles will grow fat. Some are sturdy and nearly full grown already, a few an inch or two in diameter. These barnacles, in turn, provide footing for stalked gooseneck barnacles, which sometimes grow on acorn barnacles, protruding four inches from the throat grooves, flippers, and tails of whales. One humpback may carry more than 1,000 pounds of these marine freeloaders. Almost all humpbacks have them, and although other whales carry barnacles of various species, except for gray whales in the North Pacific, no whale species has nearly as many as the humpback.

AROUND THE TIME THE FIRST HUMPBACKS ARRIVE OFF NEW England to feed—and other humpbacks turn up in the Gulf of St. Lawrence and as far north as Davis Strait, off Greenland—the right whales, ponderous as ever, lumber into Great South Channel and Massachusetts Bay to see how plentiful the copepods are. Some years, a few rights arrive as early as January; other years, many come in late April. Swimming through Massachusetts Bay, Stripe and her calf head for Cape Cod Bay, which mothers and calves prefer, perhaps for the more sheltered waters.

Rights feed differently than humpbacks. Humpbacks eat a wide range of schooling fishes, krill, and other small delicacies. Rights are more finicky. They concentrate on copepods, though they also take some juvenile krill. The

Tired of swimming and skim-feeding, a right whale lifts its head above the surface, mouth open, revealing its baleen. The baleen plates, up to eight feet long, extend far below the water line.
PHOTOGRAPH: CENTER FOR
COASTAL STUDIES

The minke whale has between 230 and
360 yellowish baleen plates, some as short
as one foot. The plates, which grow down
from the upper jaw, are made of a flexible
material much like a human fingernail.
PHOTOGRAPH: SCOTT KRAUS,
NEW ENGLAND AQUARIUM

Sand lance grow up to eight inches in length.

PHOTOGRAPH: CHARLES DOUCET

This deep-sea squid is found at a depth of 1,500 feet off Greenland. Various squid species provide food for sperm whales, pilot whales, Atlantic white-sided dolphins, and beaked whales. When young, squid feed on zooplankton. As they mature, they feed on herring, capelin, and mackerel, among other fishes.

PHOTOGRAPH: NORBERT WU

Stalked gooseneck barnacles often grow on other barnacles. They feed by waving their whiplike plumes through the water and drawing plankton toward their mouths. Gooseneck barnacles sometimes protrude four inches from the throat grooves of humpback whales.

PHOTOGRAPH: ALEX KERSTITCH

The right whale Stars, Stripe's 1981 calf, was photographed a few weeks after she became entangled, probably in a lobster-pot line. The rope slipped over her upper jaw, and the loop tightened. Despite the rope, she continues to feed and migrate every year. Many other whales die from entanglements.

PHOTOGRAPH: RACHEL BUDELSKY, NEW ENGLAND AQUARIUM

Copepods are the preferred food of right whales. A copepod is less than a quarter-inch long. It takes more than 200,000 to fill a coffee mug.

PHOTOGRAPH: NORBERT WU

copepod is a small crustacean with a round body, a pointed tail, and oarlike legs. Each copepod is less than a quarter of an inch long, and it takes more than 200,000 to fill a coffee mug. To swallow the equivalent of a coffee-mug full, Stripe would have to swim, mouth open, for a few hundred feet. Research by the Center for Coastal Studies, in Provincetown, Massachusetts, indicates that right whales like feeding areas with at least 4,000 copepods and juvenile krill per cubic meter. That is about half a teaspoon of food in a full bathtub, or a lot of swimming and food straining to get enough to eat.

Stripe finds both copepods and krill near the top of the water column. As if to get away, the copepods swim in a jerky manner, but they are not fast enough to elude Stripe. Leaving her calf for a moment, she skims just beneath the surface, mouth open, straining a particularly rich patch as she swims. Unlike the lunging, gulping humpback, the right swims through its food, mouth open. It misses nothing, filtering out the water as it goes. The water rushes in through a square-yard opening at the front of its mouth and passes through its baleen plates and out the sides of its mouth. The food, caught on the inside bristles of the baleen, is then swallowed.

Early in the season, more food can sometimes be found deep in the water column. Stripe, trailed by her calf, dives deep, mouth open, in pursuit. Down below are immature copepods and those in the process of their own migration.

The copepod migration, in early spring, is a jaunty swim from perhaps 300 feet down to near the surface. The immature male and female copepods, having spent much of the winter in the depths, swim to the surface layers to feed on fresh blooms of tasty phytoplankton. En route, many are eaten not only by right whales but also by fish, especially basking sharks, and sea birds such as petrels and phalaropes. The copepods that survive for a couple of

A right whale flips its tail high out of the water.

PHOTOGRAPH: GREGORY STONE, NEW ENGLAND AQUARIUM

months grow to maturity and mate, and the females lay fertilized eggs in the water. Three generations of copepods may live and die through a northern summer.

After hours of feeding, Stripe feels the drain of exertion and the weight of a full belly. Before taking a rest, she cleans her baleen by forcing water along the bristles and swallowing the last bits of food. Her rest, like that of most whales, is no more than a catnap, often near the surface but sometimes down below. Right whales can hold their breath for up to 25 minutes. Whales and dolphins—unlike humans and other land animals who breathe while sleeping—are voluntary breathers. They must be awake to come to the surface for air.

A right whale resting at the surface, even Stripe with the white scar on her nose, looks like a black, crusty rock being washed by a fast-moving tide—except to a keen-eyed whale researcher. On a gray, rainy day in early April, researchers from the Center for Coastal Studies see Stripe and her calf in the eerie calm of Cape Cod Bay. They approach close to take the usual identification photographs. Stripe is oblivious, apparently hearing nothing in her rocklike repose. Later that day, the researchers relay the news to Scott Kraus, of the New England Aquarium, who saw Stripe and her new calf off northern Florida in January. Pleased, Kraus dispatches an aquarium boat on April 2, to look for rights. The researchers see no sign of Stripe and her calf, but they do find Stars, one of Stripe's older calves, now mature.

A 40-foot-long, 40-ton female, Stars plows through the water, skim-feeding. She is alone this year. Last year, she became the youngest right-whale mother on record. Born in 1981, she must have mated in 1985, at age four. Previously, sexual maturity in rights was thought to occur at age seven. Stars's calf also made Stripe one of the first-known right-whale grandmothers. Yet the celebration of the event—toasted by Kraus and other right-whale researchers—was muted. Stars's calf was so small that few thought he would live, and Stars left him alone a lot while she went off to feed. The celebration was then marred by an accident. While Stars was weaning the calf, giving him daily lessons in skim-feeding, she plowed through some old fishing gear and became tangled, probably in a lobster-pot line. A loop of the rope slipped over her upper jaw and tightened when she tried to swim away. Then part of the rope wound around her tail. She broke free but was left with the loop of rope in her mouth. It fit snugly over her upper jaw and cut into the sides of her mouth like a horse's bridle and bit. No amount of thrashing in the water would dislodge it. Fortunately, her calf had stayed clear.

Throughout the rest of the summer and the early autumn of 1986, day after day, Stars stayed in Massachusetts Bay and showed her noose to hundreds of whale watchers. How could she get rid of it? The Center for Coastal Studies whale-watching and research boats saw her on 9 days in September and 15 times in the month of October—always in Massachusetts Bay. That year, there was a shortage of visiting humpbacks, which usually entertain the whale-watching crowds. Most think it was due to the sand-lance crash on Stellwagen Bank—usually the focal point for whale and human encounters in the bay. The sand lance did not eat the copepods, so there were more available for a few of the rights who arrived. The center was glad to have Stars,

Stripe, and the other rights. The rarest of all whales were for that summer right on the researchers' doorstep. And the whale watchers all wanted to help Stars.

Feeding in net-clogged coastal waters is sometimes hazardous to whale health. Three rights are known to have died in collisions with fishing gear: one in a cod trap, one in an otter trawl, and one in offshore lobster gear. The number of other whales and dolphins entangled and drowned is much higher. From 1976 to 1985, for example, more than 300 humpbacks in the North Atlantic were known to have become tangled in fishing gear, mostly cod traps and gill nets and mostly off the coast of Newfoundland. Seventy-five of these humpbacks died. Yet gill nets are a more serious problem for other sea life. Conservationists call them "walls of death" because they catch everything and anything. Gillnetters fish for marketable species such as cod or mackerel. The rest of the catch—"trash" fish, porpoises, seals, caught by the gills or the flippers and drowned—is heaved over the side. In recent years, the harbor porpoise, the smallest cetacean in the North Atlantic, has accidentally drowned by the hundreds in gill nets in the Gulf of Maine, in the Bay of Fundy, and around Newfoundland. No one knows the exact annual numbers, because fishermen in most areas rarely report the deaths, ignoring regulations that require such reports. Some researchers fear that gillnetting threatens the future of the harbor porpoise in the North Atlantic—even in its stronghold, the Bay of Fundy. In some parts of the world, gill nets have been banned, and conservationists have called for a ban off eastern Canada and New England as well. Even with a ban, however, there remain many lost or abandoned nets, called "derelict" or "ghost" nets, which lie on the bottom and continue to kill sea life for years afterward. Still, gill nets in use near the surface—sometimes left overnight, or for days in bad weather—are the most deadly for whales and dolphins.

The humpback whale Bislash opens her mouth in pursuit of sand lance, revealing past encounters with fishermen. A rope, at one time caught in her mouth, has bent and destroyed some of her baleen plates. Bislash manages to feed despite the injury but may have to take many more mouthfuls to get the same amount of food.

PHOTOGRAPH: WILLIAM ROSSITER

The flukes of humpback whales are often ragged and scarred. Some marks are from fishing nets, telling stories of previous entanglements. The parallel scars are tooth marks from killer whales, predators of whales and dolphins. Although many whales are bitten by killer whales on their flippers and flukes, most survive the attacks.

PHOTOGRAPH: WAYNE BARRETT

Some years off Newfoundland, depending on the local abundance of fish and fishermen, Jon Lien, a researcher at Memorial University, in St. John's, spends much of his time going to remote fishing villages cutting whales out of nets: mostly humpbacks, followed by minkes and fins, then pilot whales, belugas, and narwhals. Lien has saved many whales, but sometimes he is too late. One dead sperm whale he examined had 23 kinds of fishing gear in its stomach. But right whales, of all whale species, deserve the most careful monitoring because of their small population. The number of linelike scars, usually on the tail flukes, testifies to entanglement in some kind of fishing gear. Almost 60 percent of rights in the North Atlantic have such scars. Three other rights, besides Stars, carry pieces of fishing gear, all gill nets.

Stars's younger sibling, Forever, born in 1984, was caught in lobster gear when he was almost a year and a half old, soon after leaving Stripe, his mother. A lobster fisherman noticed the 30-foot-long whale struggling near Monhegan Island, Maine, and called the U.S. Coast Guard. The Coast Guard tried to cut the lobster-pot line wound around Forever's tail. But as the men

Whale researcher Jon Lien, of Memorial University of Newfoundland, releases a humpback whale trapped in a fishing net. Every year, dozens of whales become entangled in nets, especially in the waters around Newfoundland, and some die. By acting quickly and with an education program for fishermen, Lien has managed to save more and more humpbacks, as well as millions of dollars of fishing gear.

PHOTOGRAPH: BRYAN AND CHERRY ALEXANDER

The humpback whale Point shows her tail to whale watchers in Massachusetts Bay.

PHOTOGRAPH: JANE GIBBS

came close, Forever whacked his tail, barely missing the boat. Then they tried to cut the line with a 12-foot-long tree-pruning pole. They succeeded. Forever was freed and has lived perhaps to learn some caution from his misadventure. But Stars still carries her souvenir, probably to Florida each winter and back, through feeding and courting.

Back and forth in the bay, usually well below the surface but occasionally in front of whale watchers, Stars continues to skim-feed. She remains alone, apart from her mother and last year's calf, now independent. The rope chafes at the corners of her mouth, and the knot, inside her mouth, still makes her gag from time to time. So far, she has been able to feed herself. But her researcher friends wonder whether the rope will affect her chances of mating and giving birth, whether she will ever get rid of it.

THE HUMPBACK WHALE, MORE THAN ANY OTHER SPECIES, launched the whale-watching business in the North Atlantic. Even if rights were not so rare, they still tend to be too conservative. Humpbacks *perform*. They jump, lunge-feed, wave their flippers, tail-lob, and show off their reptilian profiles. Of all whales, they are the most flamboyant and the most reliable draws for tourists. They come close to shore and large population centers. They also approach whale-watching and scientific boats and seem to have a flair for the dramatic and unexpected. The meeting place for whales and humans is Stellwagen Bank, 30 miles east of Boston and 7 miles north of Provincetown, on popular Cape Cod. Most of the whale-watching companies along the Massachusetts and New Hampshire coast converge on the 18-mile-long bank. The whale-watching tours begin in mid-April, though whale watchers do not start to arrive in great numbers until May. Then there may be a dozen companies running from one to three cruises a day throughout the summer. Most cruises have a ship naturalist to tell the tourists what they are seeing and to answer questions. At the same time, the scientist does some research, recording observations and taking photographs. Thus, the tourism helps pay for the science. Many whale researchers based in New England and in eastern Canada have made arrangements with tour-boat companies, trading their expertise for valuable, expensive ship time. Other researchers run whale-watching tours themselves and use the profits to pay for their studies.

But this year, for the second year in a row, the humpbacks abandon Stellwagen Bank. Comet, twice playing the scout, swings up to take a look. Maybe next year the sand lance will return. The sand lance, other schooling fishes, and krill are more spread out in Great South Channel than has been typical on the bank, and it seems to take longer to round up a meal. Great South Channel is much farther out to sea and less protected for whales and whale-watching tours. The females Beltane and Talon, along with Talon's calf, Rush, stay busy, feeding, as the days of April lengthen and move into May. They cannot help but notice that the whale-watching boats are scarce this year.

In a cold, choppy sea in early May, one of the Dolphin fleet, a friendly whale-watching and research ship used by the Center for Coastal Studies,

Splashing its tail, a humpback whale performs off Cape Cod, Massachusetts. Humpbacks are the most reliable draws for whale watchers in the North Atlantic. Their antics have helped create a million-dollar-a-year industry.

PHOTOGRAPH: DAVID WILEY

chugs into the open waters of Great South Channel. Beltane picks up the engine sound first, a hum she has heard so many times before. The Dolphin fleet, from *Dolphin III* to *Dolphin V*, are the ships that launched whale watching in the North Atlantic in April 1975. As the ship slows to a standstill, Beltane lets the faint hum resonate pleasantly in her head while she continues setting bubble-net traps and gulping lunch. The whale watchers, led by a girl in pigtails on the aft deck, play the game of looking for the bubbles and guessing when and precisely where Beltane will come up. Every time Beltane surfaces, she is cheered by the audience. Slowly, the ship is pulled closer by the tide. It is converging on a loose group of five whales, including Crow's Nest, Shark, and New Moon. Comet, Talon, and her calf, Rush, are nearby but out of the researchers' sight. At 1:00 p.m., Beltane surfaces fairly close to the ship, arches her back, and hears a familiar voice call out, "Beltane!" Ready to take her deep dive, she flips her tail as a researcher on the boat clicks her camera. It is Carole Carlson, an American researcher long associated with the center; she has faithfully charted Beltane's movements since birth. Later that day and several times over the weekend, Beltane will meet Carlson again, as well as British researcher Phil Clapham, who several years ago came from Cornwall to find whales and stayed as director of the center's cetacean research program.

Beltane trusts the Dolphin fleet and other whale-watching boats. In 1985, with her calf, Cat Eyes, she came close to the boat, the youngster in tow, perhaps to show him off. But even without a calf, she is friendly.

On May 2, Beltane surfaces again, and whale watchers photograph her many times on the long day cruise. On May 3, Beltane appears with Crow's Nest and Pump. This time, they make for the boat. Beltane is curious and friendly. She hears the screams of whale watchers through the hull as she cruises underneath the boat. Just below the water's surface floats the ghostly image of Beltane's long white flippers. Then she raises her head and cracks the image to breathe. Clapham looks out at her knobby snout and curious eye. He can almost see the hair on each bump on Beltane's snout, like the small hair that grows out of moles. He is elated once again by the antics of this old friend.

Still in the front row on the aft deck, the girl with the pigtails, having met Beltane, is ecstatic. She has been waiting for this chance since she saw a television show on whales two years ago. Falling in love with their graceful beauty, she thought, "What if I could meet a whale?" The ones on the TV were sleek and elegant blue whales. The humpbacks, featuring Beltane, seem like ugly cousins at first. Nonetheless, they win her over. They are so big and alive; they are wild, yet they come so close. These ugly whales have winning ways. They can even sing. Beltane lifts her long head out of the water and gazes up at her audience before returning to the business of the day: eating. The girl—and Phil Clapham—will long remember this instant of contact. Humans and whales have shared a moment of wonder about the other.

A humpback whale surfaces at dawn near the *Halos*, the research ship of the Center for Coastal Studies, after an all-night study session. A new day of whale watching and research begins.

PHOTOGRAPH: WILLIAM ROSSITER

# BEHOLD AN ANIMAL

*that is an essay in power and size, a sleek,*
*muscular model of evolution's ultimate engineering.*

# SUMMER

**S**UMMER COMES LATE to most of the Gulf of St. Lawrence. Compared with New England, the St. Lawrence has only a brief, soggy interlude of spring that is best described as the great meltdown. When summer finally arrives, propelled by the long days of the northern latitudes of Québec, it almost trips on the heels of winter. The ice cover, sometimes lingering into June, cracks and crunches, tapping out rhythms as it melts. At the northeast corner of the gulf, the 10-mile-wide Strait of Belle Isle is an often ice-choked passage between Labrador and Newfoundland. Here, a harp seal, prolonging its northward migration, can relax at the ice edge at midnight on the longest day of the year and gaze out at the open North Atlantic Ocean and watch icebergs drift by.

As the ice melts, far below the frozen surface, the fish begin to spawn, laying their eggs on the sea floor. The fish time spawning so that their soon-to-hatch young will have their favorite plankton available at just the right size for eating. First to spawn, in April, are

American plaice, which have spent the long winter in the deep waters of the gulf. By May, the spring run of herring arrives from its over-wintering grounds south of Newfoundland and on the Scotian Shelf. In late May, capelin—a smaller, slimmer cold-water version of herring—swim in from the open North Atlantic in dense schools. The capelin will spawn throughout much of the summer, taking advantage of the copepods and the krill along the north shore of the St. Lawrence estuary and gulf.

The plankton explosion of the north shore can be traced to the rushing water from a deep trench called the Laurentian Trough. It begins 150 miles out at sea, out along the continental slope south of Newfoundland, and extends to the northwest, to the gulf. The trough draws a massive inflow of seawater into the gulf from the North Atlantic. This salty "submarine river" winds through Cabot Strait, crosses the gulf, and upwells along the north shore. The biggest upwellings occur in places where the forces of tides, the outpouring St. Lawrence River, and the sudden changes in bottom topography conspire to drive the seawater toward the surface. With it come the nutrients on which plankton thrive. Among the most productive marine regions of the North Atlantic, the north shore, with its upwellings, is unique in one important way: it reliably draws the world's biggest eater, the great blue whale—*Balaenoptera musculus.*

Tail flukes moving up and down, blood pumping furiously, an 80-foot-long female blue whale named June races into the gulf, hunger gnawing in her multichambered stomach. Her stomach is the size of a small blimp. Behold an animal that is an essay in power and size, a sleek, muscular model of evolution's ultimate engineering. Yet the largest animal that, as far as is known, has ever lived on Earth—two or three times the size of the largest dinosaurs—is dependent utterly on some of the smallest animals on Earth, several species of zooplankton known as krill, no more than an inch and a half long.

Passing through Cabot Strait, around the southwest tip of Newfoundland, June tastes the krill, bit patches here and there, but she still drives on, knowing that when she reaches the promised land of upwellings along the north shore of the Gulf of St. Lawrence, the krill will be thick. Thick enough to make it worth her while to travel this far. Up, down, up, down, her flukes move.

But she feels so tired. Last winter, June carried a calf, gave birth, nursed, then migrated. In January, when Junior was born, he measured 23 feet in length and weighed 5,500 pounds. June was almost plump then, living off her blubber, but the nursing has taken its toll. Junior needs more than 50 gallons of milk a day. He is growing at a furious rate, putting on about 200 pounds a day, or 8 pounds an hour. June feels that she is losing weight faster than he is putting it on! The calf, now five months old, has increased to five or six times his birth weight. At age eight months, when he leaves June later in the summer, he will be about 50 feet long and will weigh 50,000 pounds. He will be longer than a full-grown humpback or right whale and almost as heavy. When he reaches sexual maturity, at more than 10 years old, he may exceed 75 feet and weigh perhaps 100 tons. But he will never be as big as his mother. Female blues are larger than males. The record size for a female blue,

*Page 45:*
The sky breaks after a spell of foul weather.
PHOTOGRAPH: RICHARD SEARS,
MINGAN ISLAND CETACEAN STUDY

A blue whale spouts as it breaks the surface. Viewed in an aerial survey, blues look almost small, but this mature blue may be 85 feet long. Blues, because of the mottled patterns on their backs, tend to take on the bluish-gray color of the sea and sky.

PHOTOGRAPH: RICHARD SEARS,
MINGAN ISLAND CETACEAN STUDY

caught in the Antarctic some decades ago, was about 100 feet and 150 tons.

June presses on, her big calf trailing, swimming with all his might and ever more insistent when hungry for milk. Pushing his mouth against the underside of his mother in motion, he can activate the jets of high-fat milk. But June is weaning him. It is nurse on the run or not at all. Junior takes it on the run. June, slowed though not stopped by his nursing, will show him how to eat solids the minute they arrive at the first good feeding grounds. He will learn the art of catching wily krill.

Krill look like tiny shrimp, save for their bristled tails. Alert animals, they have good eyesight and can swim with dexterity, avoiding slower-moving whales and fish. Most baleen whales eat some krill, but none depend on krill as much as the blue. The speed of a blue whale enhances its ability to make the catch. The first thing krill notice with a blue whale is also the last thing they see—a cavernous mouth closing in on them and thousands of other hapless zooplankton swirling around in a torrent of rushing water.

While June, Junior, and other blues swim in from the open ocean, the krill devour the spring blooms of phytoplankton that follow the ice break-up. Most of the krill are nearly a year old, though a few are two-year-old survivors. The previous July or two Julys ago, the parents of these krill released eggs after mating. The larvae grew quickly during the summer, then took a breather during the winter freeze-up. As soon as the sun thawed the ice and the phytoplankton began to bloom in the upper surface layers, the krill came up to feed. By late spring, they were mature. With any luck, they mate before the blue whales arrive.

Krill are found throughout the world ocean, especially in cold water. There are many species, ranging in size from less than one-quarter of an inch to almost two and a half inches. The largest is *Euphausia superba*, found in the southern ocean. Also shown is *Stylocheiron maximum*.

PHOTOGRAPH: NORBERT WU

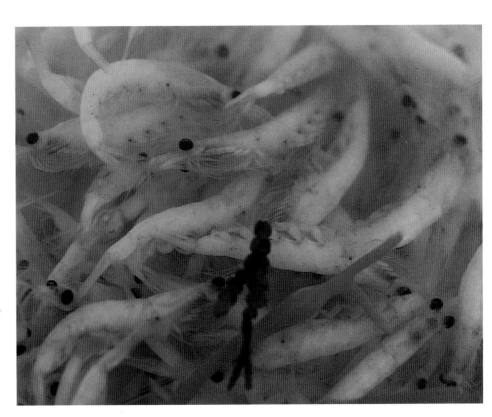

Krill, or euphausiids, are shrimplike crustaceans of the order Euphausiacea. Humpback, fin, minke, and right whales eat some krill, but blue whales subsist on them. A blue eats four or more tons of krill a day. Arctic krill of two species, each about one and a half inches long, are the most important in the diet of blue and other whales in the North Atlantic.

PHOTOGRAPH: DOTTE LARSEN

A blue whale gulps krill and water, perhaps 40 to 50 tons in a single mouthful the size of a large living room. For a few minutes, until it expels the water, the blue almost doubles its weight.

PHOTOGRAPH: DOC WHITE

On June 20, June and her calf sweep past Anticosti Island and roar into the home stretch, the krill growing thicker by the mile. The thickest patches are at least 300 feet down. On the surface, the stiff black sea is whipped to a froth by 20-knot winds. June suddenly dives deep, leaving the calf in her bubbles to watch in wonder. She picks up speed as she turns, tail moving up and down. Then, driving toward the surface, she opens her mouth as wide as she can. Her throat pleats expand, and filling with water and krill, her "pouch" bulges, stretching to several times its size. This expanding pouch is common to most baleen whales, including the humpback, but its pouch does not expand nearly so much. A blue-whale pouch holds from 40 to 50 tons or more of water and krill. With one mouthful, June can almost double her weight—at least for a few minutes. The load, however, is mostly water. Now comes the tricky part: June has to swallow the food and expel the water.

June, with her jaws and back straining from the weight, lets the momentum of her charge carry her up toward the surface. As she ascends, she turns on her back and arcs it so that the pouch itself is the first thing to break the surface. She opens her mouth slightly, and the water rushes out through her baleen. With the help of gravity, she rolls onto her side while more water spills out. Now on her belly, she spouts—a thick, towering spray—and takes a deep breath. For a few minutes, she continues swimming and surfacing and straining until only food remains. A swallow or two, and the reward is safely stowed. Then, after a glance at her calf, she goes for another mouthful. And another and another. June seems obsessed with eating. She relaxes a bit when she finds her stride, but she will maintain this pace throughout most of the summer. June must eat four or more tons of krill each day. She is the role model for her calf Junior, and this is her lesson: eat and eat fast, for tomorrow it is winter.

FAR TO THE SOUTH OF THE ST. LAWRENCE, IN THE GULF OF Maine, which extends from Nova Scotia to Cape Cod Bay, summer is normally a much more leisurely affair. Without ice to contend with, the humpback whales Comet, Beltane, Talon, and Rush can settle in, eating steadily but taking time to play and enjoy the scenery. Stripe, Stripe's calf, Stars, and most of the other North Atlantic right whales also feed in ice-free areas, though they are slower in their movements and more methodical in their feeding habits.

But many humpbacks—and occasionally some rights—feed in the Gulf of St. Lawrence. At one time, before the whaling era, the gulf was filled with both species. On the breeding grounds in the Caribbean, the Gulf of Maine humpbacks such as Comet and Torch mix with the St. Lawrence humpbacks. The St. Lawrence whales travel about 2,000 miles more every year to feed. There are fewer of them, and they have more area, and more food, to themselves.

Whales adopt feeding areas probably through habit or through the influence of their mother. The right whales seen in the St. Lawrence in September 1976—the only sighting on the north shore of the gulf in this century—may have been searching for long-lost feeding grounds. Once in a

A humpback whale lunge-feeds in the Gulf of St. Lawrence. In the North Atlantic, humpbacks tend to have favorite feeding grounds, anywhere from the Cape Cod area to Greenland, probably through the influence of their mother. Some humpbacks, however, break the rules, changing feeding grounds from year to year or even in a single season.

PHOTOGRAPH: RICHARD SEARS,
MINGAN ISLAND CETACEAN STUDY

while, of course, whales switch feeding grounds for a year or two, or they visit new ones. It is usually hunger that drives them—as in the case of Comet and his companions, who recently abandoned Stellwagen Bank for Great South Channel—though sometimes it appears to be mere whim.

To humpback- and right-whale researchers, a highlight of the summer of 1987 is the visit of a blue whale to the waters around Cape Cod. This mature whale, named Cosmo, was seen in the northern Gulf of St. Lawrence in August of the previous two summers. In the middle of the summer of 1987, however, Cosmo decides to visit the waters off Gloucester, Massachusetts. The humpback Beltane, checking out Jeffreys Ledge, sees Cosmo. She does a double take, then stops feeding. Days later, the right whale Stars encounters Cosmo. The great blue is a magnificent sight, perhaps even to another whale unaccustomed to seeing an animal so fast, sleek, and long. But Cosmo has a problem. A round green fishing buoy—the kind used by gillnetters—is firmly hooked to his left flipper. Stars, with the rope still looped around her upper jaw, stares at the big whale, also humbled by man. Comet, Beltane, and Talon are a little more familiar with the heavy ship traffic in the area. As curious as they are at times, they are fairly careful to avoid fishing gear. A few days later, in Cape Cod Bay, researchers of the Center for Coastal Studies see the big blue, still with the buoy. The rare sighting is diminished by the animal's mishap.

ON THE MORNING OF JUNE 15, OFF THE SOUTH SHORE OF New Jersey, three bottlenose dolphins surf in the high, breaking waves resulting from yesterday's stiff northeaster. Part of a much larger school in late winter, these dolphins travelled on migration with the humpbacks Beltane, Talon, and Rush and even ran into Stripe and her new calf off North Carolina.

A humpback whale is escorted by Atlantic white-sided dolphins. The two species, sometimes joined by fin and minke whales, often feed together on small schooling fishes.

PHOTOGRAPH: WILLIAM ROSSITER

An Atlantic white-sided dolphin spouts—a quick puff from its blowhole—as it cracks the surface alongside the bow of a boat. These seven- to nine-foot-long dolphins are found only in the North Atlantic. Like many dolphin species, they are high spirited—leaping, breaching, tail-lobbing, and bow-riding.

PHOTOGRAPH: WILLIAM ROSSITER

Bottlenose dolphins, in the act of feeding, sometimes chase fish onto the shore and beach themselves. They catch the fish, then wriggle back into the water.

PHOTOGRAPH: LOUIS RIGLEY

Bottlenose dolphins leap in play. Present throughout much of the world ocean, they prefer warm temperate waters in the North Atlantic. An inshore population ranges from Florida in winter to New Jersey in summer.

PHOTOGRAPH: INTERNATIONAL FUND FOR ANIMAL WELFARE

Their migration paths, however, only briefly coincided. Bottlenose dolphins prefer warmer water, but in 1987, the water, even off New Jersey, where they like to spend the summer, seems almost tropical. They whistle such things back and forth to each other in stinging high-pitched bursts of sound. They leap high in the air. This is *fun!* For days, they have been feeding on schools of flounder, ling, and other common offshore fishes, and now they are full, and ready for anything.

This surfing is a bit of pure nonsense, like a bow ride on the waves of a passing ship. When there is a lot of food and some spare time, it is pleasant. But today, as the long waves roll in along the New Jersey shore, surfing is a chore. Again, as in recent days, the dolphins are having difficulty breathing. They stop and lie on the water, taking an early rest. First one, then another. The sun, shining on their backs, reveals peeling skin on two of the dolphins, a female and her calf, plus raw lesions on a third, a young male. The three animals, more tired than they have ever felt before, try to rest and ride it out. Maybe a catnap will help. As they bob in the waves, the swells from yesterday's storm grow fatter, the troughs longer. The undulating motion is hypnotic as the current carries the dolphins ever closer to the shallows. The calf wakes up and manages to nudge his mother before they hit the beach. Summoning all their energy, they push off, into deeper water. The young male is aware that they are leaving but has no more strength to fight. He lets the waves carry him onto the beach. He sinks into the sand, washed by the outgoing tide.

He waits, an hour, two, three, well into midday. His skin is peeling more, his lesions festering. His back is burning; his insides are cooking. He is almost delirious from the pain, taking it in cycles of dozing, waiting, writhing. His mouth is parched. He is dying of thirst. He can barely manage to whistle. Another hour passes. Then the young male feels something on his back, a touch. He hears soft words. He opens an eye and sees a man. The shadow of the man momentarily shields his hot back from the sun. The relief of contact, even for an instant, is exquisite. Then, with a sigh that begins with a bit of pleasure through the pain, the life goes out.

The man, Bob Schoelkopf, was trying to help the dolphin. After the dolphin dies, his mission is to find out what went wrong. He takes the dolphin to the Marine Mammal Stranding Center in nearby Brigantine, New Jersey, for a necropsy. As director of the center, he makes sure that his research team keeps some of the organs and tissues, freezing them for later analysis. A few days later, Schoelkopf picks up the dead male's companions, the female and then the calf, farther down the beach. There are more in the days to come, including a dead spotted dolphin and a sick bottlenose, which he brings back to the center. Three minutes after the sick bottlenose is placed in the center's rehabilitation pool, he dies.

When Schoelkopf and his team open up the dolphins, they find fluid build-up in the lungs, "as though the dolphins had inhaled some type of toxic irritant." Concerned, Schoelkopf flies an aerial survey over the southern New Jersey coast. He flies over miles and miles of sunbathers on one of the world's busiest beaches, then dips and turns and heads out to sea. About five miles off the coast, he sees a track of garbage and turns to follow it. Parallel to the beach, the track extends for 60 miles. Sharks are feeding on the garbage, but there is so much that it will not simply disappear. Some of it is inedible plastic waste.

IN THE GULF OF ST. LAWRENCE, THE BLUE WHALES JUNE AND Junior seem far from any pollution. Midday on June 22, they are feeding in a flat-calm sea on the north shore near the Mingan Islands of Québec. They hear the putts and whines of an outboard engine drawing ever closer. From a distance through the haze, their tall, unmistakable blue-whale spouts have revealed their presence. The calf is frightened, and June knows some of the same fear. But the boat does not come too near. Two researchers, Martine Bérubé and Diane Gendron, ride close to the water in an inflatable boat that is only half the length of Junior. They slow the engine and pull up 150 feet away to watch. June decides that they are "friendly" humans, and she resumes feeding.

Bérubé and Gendron motor near to the spot where they think June will surface. They wait. Junior comes up for brief spouts, then starts speed-swim-

A blue whale lifts its flukes, perhaps 20 feet across, before diving deep. Unlike humpback whales, which commonly "fluke," only 18 percent of blues in the St. Lawrence raise their tails on a regular basis. A blue may stay down for as long as 20 minutes.

PHOTOGRAPH: RICHARD SEARS, MINGAN ISLAND CETACEAN STUDY

ming at the surface, distracting the researchers' attention. Junior is imitating his mother's food-gulping bursts. But he is also excited by the strangers. He turns toward the boat and, a few seconds later, dives down, swimming below it and looking up at its boxlike silhouette. June gives the calf free rein. Still hungry, June disappears, diving for krill deep in the water column. She stays down for at least 11 minutes, according to the researchers' count. Then *whoosh!* She spouts, and as she arches her back, Gendron and Bérubé snap photographs. Researchers are usually able to take only one or two photographs of whales at a time, but blues are so long that they keep rolling through the water. With a motor-drive camera, a researcher can manage half a dozen or more shots of a blue. Finally, June's tiny dorsal fin comes into view, and they take the most important photograph. This picture, with the fin as a reference point, will allow the researchers to make a map of June's back. Just as a humpback can be identified by the markings on its tail and a right by the callosity patterns on its head, a blue can be recognized by the mottled patterns on its back.

The researchers photograph both sides of June, then leave to visit other whale species in the area. They find 16 fin whales, including an old fin friend, Curley; 5 minke whales, the smallest of the baleen whales; and a rambunctious young male humpback, Jigsaw. Jigsaw is making the first of many appearances this season. Fellow humpbacks Comet and Torch know Jigsaw, and they have all sung and scuffled together on the mating grounds, but Jigsaw prefers the feeding grounds he has visited since birth.

There are several feeding areas in the St. Lawrence, determined mainly by the availability of food. Blue whales prefer the deepest water, at 300 feet or more, 1 to 15 miles from shore. Some of the humpbacks, fins, and minkes feed there, too—and sometimes on krill. But these three species generally

A fin whale breaches in a white-capped sea. At 60 to 70 feet long, fins are the second largest whale. Only the right side of the jaw is white—a characteristic of all fin whales.

PHOTOGRAPH: CENTER FOR COASTAL STUDIES

Two fin whales roll through the waters of the northern Gulf of St. Lawrence. Fins feed in tight groups of half a dozen, mostly on schooling fishes and krill.

PHOTOGRAPH: RICHARD SEARS,
MINGAN ISLAND CETACEAN STUDY

feed in shallower water. The minkes, in fact, are almost on the beach, in an area researchers call Minke Way. The three smaller whales prefer the little schooling fishes, such as capelin, that come inshore. When capelin spawn close to shore, humpbacks, fins, and minkes go a bit crazy. The capelin arrive in great schools after spending a year at sea, usually at night in the summer. Spent, they are easy prey for whales; they hardly have time to eat their krill.

At the research station, a rambling house in a Québec fishing village, Martine Bérubé phones program leader Richard Sears. He is the founder of the Mingan Island Cetacean Study, set up in 1979 to research blue and other baleen whales in the St. Lawrence. Sears, who will arrive a week later, is dismayed to learn that he has missed a rare chance to see a blue calf still with its mother. In 1980, he photographically identified a mother named Bulleta travelling with a calf. The following year, he ran across Bulleta again and, as expected, found her alone. Blue-whale mothers are thought to spend only about eight months with their calves, before the youngsters venture out on their own.

Sears encountered Bulleta again and again in later years, but there was no new calf. This was not encouraging for a species reduced to a tiny percentage of its original population. Blue whales are thought to have numbered about 300,000 worldwide before whalers began hunting them a century ago. There are now an estimated 5,000. Sears believes that as few as several hundred live in the North Atlantic. The only known hangout for any part of the year, the place where they can be reliably found, is along the north shore of the Gulf of St. Lawrence. Sears and his team have photo-identified 217 blues, but only 20 percent of those are considered regulars, having returned to the area for three or more years. Some 80 percent of the whales they have identified are wide-ranging roamers.

IN EARLY JULY, MORE BOTTLENOSE DOLPHINS, TOGETHER with a surprising number of sea turtles, wash ashore on the New Jersey coast, and holiday-goers begin to take notice. For Bob Schoelkopf or anyone else, walking the beaches is no longer pleasant. Dolphins have always washed up along the New Jersey shore, but at the rate of two or three a year, not half a dozen in one month. In the past, the cause of death has been old age, disease, or shark attack. On July 14, as the death toll reaches seven, Schoelkopf calls the National Marine Fisheries Service, the U.S. government agency in charge of managing marine mammals. Within two weeks, as more dolphins beach along the coast from New Jersey to Virginia Beach, Virginia, including at several resorts, the U.S. Department of Commerce authorizes a full investigation. The department appoints Joseph R. Geraci as principal investigator. He is a specialist in marine-mammal husbandry and disease from the University of Guelph, in Ontario. Geraci organizes a multidisciplinary team of pathologists at leading universities to work with government biologists and technicians to try to solve the mystery through pathology, virology, bacteriology, serology, and toxicology.

By the end of July, in New Jersey, 33 dolphins have beached themselves; 33 more strand in August. The multimillion-dollar tourism industry is in trouble. Besides the dolphins, sludge washes up, then medical waste in the

A bottlenose dolphin dies on a New Jersey beach.
PHOTOGRAPH: MICHAEL BAYTOFF

form of syringes and intravenous bags. Swimmers complain of sickness. The headlines read, "DON'T GO NEAR THE WATER" and "BEWARE: DOLPHIN AIDS." East-coast beaches attract some 10 million people on any summer weekend day, but by mid-August, the line of cars on the road to Atlantic City leads away from the beach. What is wrong? One theory is that the dolphins may have some sort of plague. Is it AIDS? Could it have been passed through the medical waste in the water? Can it be passed back to humans? The State of New Jersey must act now.

The New Jersey Department of Health determines that the number of reported cases of sick swimmers through the summer of 1987 fits the average. The complaints can be explained by the usual stomach troubles of tourists on holiday anywhere. The New Jersey Department of Environmental Protection tests inshore and offshore waters. Staff dye the effluent from city outflow pipes along the shore and watch it disperse far and wide. They determine that the water is safe for swimming. Still, the governor details a 14-point plan of action to clean up beaches and waters. Bills on ocean dumping and effluent are put on the agenda of state and provincial lawmakers all along the Atlantic seaboard, from eastern Canada to the southern United States.

But what about the dolphins? As Geraci's team, working in laboratories as far away as Miami, Florida, and Halifax, Nova Scotia, begin their work, the carcasses continue to pile up. In August, at least 125 dolphins strand along the Virginia coast. About 80 are examined as part of the clinical investigation, with tissues sent for tests for heavy metals, organochlorine compounds such as PCBs, other toxic residues, viruses, and even biological toxins. To find out whether the dolphins have AIDS, the U.S. Center for Disease Control runs tests. The results are negative.

Could the dolphins have eaten something that was contaminated? Could they have inhaled a toxic gas? Do the deaths have anything to do with ocean dumping and marine pollution in general? Did the persistent northeast winds and warm eddies of the Gulf Stream of 1987, responsible for bringing in the garbage, deliver a toxin to the dolphins? Answers would have to wait for more science.

RICHARD SEARS VENTURES OUT OFF OLD FORT BAY, QUEBEC, near the Strait of Belle Isle, 300 miles northeast of the research station in the Mingan Islands. It is early August, and the weather is rough. By afternoon, however, the sea turns calm, and as Sears heads west, he runs into Backbar, an easy-going mature 75-foot-long blue whale, probably male. Backbar was first encountered in 1980 and has been seen many times since. And today's encounter is the first of many this year. In two weeks, Sears, back in the Mingan Islands, spots Backbar again. A month later, Backbar will be seen feeding off Sept-Iles, Québec, 100 miles west of the Mingan Islands. Even later, Backbar will return to the Mingan Islands with two other long-time friends and intrepid travellers—the ice-scarred blues Pita and Hagar. These are the only movements that researchers can document, just a partial record. In fact, Backbar and the others crisscross the north shore of the Gulf of St. Lawrence almost weekly on their summer and autumn rounds: they are fully at home in the gulf.

Probably more than any other whale, blues are true nomads. To a blue, the North Atlantic is a small place. Blue whales are so quick, so large, and so contemptuous of space and distance that to them the Gulf of St. Lawrence is little more than a pond. They appear to travel singly or in pairs, yet dozens of blues, though well spaced, will appear on a feeding ground at the same time. On the grand scale of blues, this group could be travelling together. To even consider such an idea, however, let alone document such natural history, is a feat in itself. Yet this young Canadian-American research team has adapted to blues and their nomadic lifestyle. Sears and his team must stay in top physical condition to keep up with blues, to withstand the spine-numbing bounces of a small inflatable boat in often-rough seas. Dressed in their matching orange survival suits, they ambush whales, take their photographs, and maintain tight surveillance in conditions that would have movie stuntmen demanding doubles.

But in the summer of 1987, even Sears's daredevil team cannot keep up with June and her calf. June's krill-eating lessons are proceeding well, and Junior is eating more and more. Yet every few days, June must find a new feeding area. This means that during the trip, Junior will resume nursing and slow them down. Two more months of this. But the calf must experience the feeding grounds, must learn where things are and what is required in the season of non-stop eating.

Swimming hard and fast now, the water rushing against him, the calf wonders where he and June are going. Surfacing, he can see, for the first time, land on both sides of him. They are in the St. Lawrence River, and they are swimming upstream. The force of the current against them is intense at times. But June shows Junior how to swim down deep to find the cold, clean bottom currents that are moving upriver. The cold water seems to numb their tired fluke muscles. Two days later, riding the upwelling currents, they float up from a deep underwater canyon where the Saguenay River meets the St. Lawrence. Above them, in the water column, are storm clouds of reddish-brown krill. The clouds are so dense and dark that the bright, shimmery surface, a sunny day shining through the upper water layers, turns to pin pricks of light. First June opens her mouth, then Junior imitates her. They come up, almost side by side, in a *whoosh* that scatters birds at the surface and sends them screaming. The whales do their arc-and-roll feeding. Arc, arc, expel water, roll, expel more water, then swallow krill. Repeat. Gradually, the calf is getting it. The krill taste different here. The water *is* different. There are different nutrients, and some of them are of dubious vintage. The St. Lawrence River at times reminds the whales of polluted areas of the east coast of North America, the areas near port cities and around dumping grounds, the areas they usually avoid. They might avoid the St. Lawrence, too, but there is *so* much food.

The river pollution comes from Chicago, Detroit, Windsor, Cleveland, Buffalo, Toronto, Montréal, millions of people, and shipping traffic on the Great Lakes. Some of the more dangerous contaminants come from aluminum plants on the Saguenay River of Québec. The north-shore upwellings, however, lessen the impact of the pollution. The clean incoming bottom water flushes out the gulf and the mouth of the St. Lawrence River,

Belugas, or white whales, are Arctic mammals that spend most of the year in and around ice. In summer, they swim thousands of miles up rivers. Fewer than 500 of these whales reside year-round in the St. Lawrence River and estuary. Already reduced by overhunting and dams, the beluga population in the St. Lawrence is declining further as a result of pollution.
PHOTOGRAPH: FLIP NICKLIN

Blue whales, only part-time visitors to the
St. Lawrence River, have avoided most of
the ill effects of pollution.
PHOTOGRAPH: RICHARD SEARS,
MINGAN ISLAND CETACEAN STUDY

A fin whale surfaces in Halifax harbor.
PHOTOGRAPH: HAL WHITEHEAD

diluting or removing some of the pollution, and gives life a chance. The St. Lawrence is by far the largest river system on the east coast of North America—equal to all the other east-coast rivers combined. Yet, like more and more of the freshwater systems on Earth, its future is tarnished by what continues to flow into it.

Blue whales, always on the move and only part-time visitors to the river, have avoided most of the ill effects of pollution. Another whale, a toothed species called the beluga, or white whale, has not been so fortunate. These Arctic whales are up to 15 feet in length, and they live in the river year-round, lonely survivors of a time 10,000 to 12,000 years ago when the lower St. Lawrence was part of the cold Champlain Sea. The bones of bowhead whales and numerous Arctic seals, dating from this period, have been found in building excavations in downtown Ottawa and Montréal. When the glaciers of the last ice age retreated, these belugas were cut off from the Arctic, where all the other belugas live. They adapted well to life in the river—until humans came. The beluga population in the St. Lawrence, as recently as a century ago, was thought to be 5,000. Today, there are only 450 to 500, due to overhunting, habitat loss from dams, and pollution.

Pierre Béland and Daniel Martineau, Québec researchers specializing in toxicology and pathology, have established the St. Lawrence National Institute of Ecotoxicology, a research group dedicated to the St. Lawrence beluga. Since 1982, they have retrieved most of the 72 belugas that have died. When

No humpback whale leaves the feeding grounds in the Gulf of Maine before the summer-autumn feast is over.

PHOTOGRAPH: JANE GIBBS

a call comes into their laboratory in Rimouski, they drop everything and head out by car and by boat. They bring the carcass to the laboratory for a necropsy. They measure contaminants in the tissues and the organs. So far, every beluga has been "highly contaminated." They have found 24 potentially toxic contaminants, everything from PCBs and DDT to lead and mercury. They have found belugas with tumors, bladder cancers, and herpes-like skin lesions. Some belugas have had such high contaminant levels that under certain government regulations, they would be considered hazardous waste. Only about 20 to 30 belugas are born each year in the St. Lawrence, about half the birthrate of belugas in the Arctic. As the St. Lawrence beluga population slowly declines, Béland and Martineau, with beluga researcher Leone Pippard, are fighting for the beluga's right to clean water. Industry has in recent years begun to realize the plight of the beluga and has even helped sponsor conferences. Yet a few hundred belugas are not going to stop aluminum and other industries worth billions of dollars from pouring billions of gallons of this and that into the river. Or at least they are not likely to stop the dumping in time.

After a few days of bumping into the ghostly belugas in the river, June and Junior are on the prowl again in the gulf. Junior is beginning to recognize places that he visited earlier in the season. The feeding grounds are becoming home. In a rich krill patch somewhere in the gulf, June and Junior grow apart. They never really bid goodbye: they simply drift away from each other. Junior will remember his mother, but he will no longer need her or seek her out. He is so hungry! His greatest joy is swallowing krill. And June needs all her time now to put on blubber for the winter. She has done her job: because of her, the species has a better chance of survival.

Her next encounter with the blue-whale researchers is on September 17 in the Mingan Islands, 300 miles away. She is businesslike and offers no clue that she has abandoned Junior. Sears and his team spend the morning with a great herd of Atlantic white-sided dolphins—some 300 of them—all in a mile-and-a-half circle, breaching, speed-swimming, tail-slapping, and flushing herring out of the water as they go. Later, the researchers meet a big group of fin whales. Next, June appears alone, and the team does not recognize her without Junior. Then a young fin whale comes over and chases the blue for four breaths. June does a double take. Is Junior back? No, just a lonely, curious, or perhaps confused fin whale. Fins and blues are closely related whale species. The fin whales are just a few feet smaller and thus are the second largest animal on Earth.

June dives deep to elude the fin whale. It is only later, when the photographs are developed, that the researchers realize that it was June and that Junior must have separated from her. It fits the known timetable of blue-whale calves leaving their mothers, at about eight months. The researchers hope that they will see Junior again soon. Maybe he will become an old friend, one of the regular returning blue whales of the Gulf of St. Lawrence.

THE FULL BLOOM OF SUMMER COMES TO NORTH ATLANTIC waters, from the Gulf of Maine to the Gulf of St. Lawrence, at different times. By mid-August, however, most areas are at their peak. The abundant phytoplankton from early summer have made krill and copepods plentiful. Life explodes in all directions and all the way up the food chain. The explosion reverberates into October and even November, and no whale—humpback, right, or blue—leaves before the banquet is over. No whale researcher leaves, either: for sun and sea and abundance of whales, this is the most enjoyable part of the year.

Yet this year, the unexplained deaths of bottlenose dolphins off the U.S. east coast, from Virginia to New Jersey, weigh heavily on the minds of all whale and dolphin researchers. Of the whales, the humpbacks Comet, Beltane, Talon, and Rush, feeding most of the summer in Great South Channel, are closest to the area, some 300 miles by sea. They are unaware, however, that some of the dolphins they met briefly on migration last spring are now dead. As the dolphin death toll climbs week by week, the total reaches several hundred, and researchers privately wonder how many more animals—dolphins and perhaps other whale species—are dying quietly at sea, never to be counted. Will their study animals be next? In September, the monthly death toll of dolphins is less than in August, but it is still high. All agree that the bottlenose dolphins along the east coast of North America, thought to have numbered about 1,500, have suffered a crushing blow. Reports leak out that some of the carcasses are riddled with PCBs—oily synthetic toxic compounds used as lubricants and in refrigeration and insulation. They were banned in the United States in 1979, but unable to break down, they linger in the environment. PCBs cause reproductive failure in animals and suppress their immune systems. But no one knows whether the dolphins are dying from ingestion of PCBs or any other contaminant, whether pollution has provoked this mass slaughter. As more dolphins wash ashore, researchers continue to look for answers.

Humpback whales feed in the eerie light of a smoggy sunset over Boston, Massachusetts.

PHOTOGRAPH: CENTER FOR
COASTAL STUDIES

BLOWING, BREATHING, AND DIVING,
*they move rhythmically in a line,
a grand procession that celebrates life.*

# AUTUMN

**T**IDES, EBBING AND FLOWING, have the power to confound and the ability to surprise. Tides can so change the character of a shoreline that even experienced mariners sometimes lose their bearings and forget navigational hazards. Beachcombers find themselves rolling up their trousers, dangerously surrounded by water.

Tides are intensely local affairs. Tide tables, made up from past tides in specific areas, are less reliable for a given place and time than even one sharp-eyed old woman who watches the sea out of her window. Tides will cast on a shoreline all manner of things, plastic and organic, living and dead. The ultimate tidal surprise is a whale. Most whales know tides, feeding along tide rips and respecting them, though deepwater species, unaccustomed to gently sloping beaches, are sometimes caught off guard, and strand. For example, tides have delivered to researchers several species of deep-sea beaked whales that have never before been seen. Increasingly in recent years, tides have also brought in whales that are well known to researchers, whales that have died quietly at sea. Some are even individuals known by name.

Tides are caused by the gravitational pull of the moon and the sun. The moon's gravity has greater impact on the Earth because the moon is closer. The sun's gravity is independent in its effect; it merely enhances or diminishes the moon's. As the moon revolves around the Earth, it pulls at the planet's surface. Not much occurs on the inflexible surface of the land. But in the ocean, the water rises in a mass directly below the moon. As the Earth rotates, the huge lump of water jolts into the land, piles up, and then recedes.

Nothing so simple, however, can explain the tides in the Bay of Fundy, among the most diabolical in the world. They can turn into swirling, roiling monsters. The rip tides and whirlpools even have names. Old Sow Whirlpool, offshore near the Canada–United States border between New Brunswick and Maine, can tilt and spin a 60-foot-long fishing boat in its 4-foot vortex. In the northernmost part of the bay, tides may rise and fall by as much as 55 feet in 12 hours. By contrast, a few hundred miles south, at Nantucket Island, off Cape Cod, the tides rise and fall rarely more than 3 feet.

Geography accounts for much of the movement in the Bay of Fundy. Located at the edge of a basin, the bay is a long, narrow water trough. Incoming cold-water tides turn the corner at Cape Sable Island, off Nova Scotia's southern tip. They pour into the trough, sloshing against the sides and sending water far up the beaches. In addition, there are broken, jagged rocks—underwater mountains, cliffs, and canyons—along the bottom of the trough, and there are islands—Grand Manan, Campobello, and The Wolves. The water streams around the islands and catches in the jagged underwater rocks, then shoots up or drives at odd angles, causing strange currents to develop. The offshoot is some unpredictable weather, including fog, which sometimes moves in for days.

There is one benefit from this fierce tidal action: it keeps nutrients in the water column, making them available to phytoplankton and zooplankton. Although it does not keep them as high in the water column as the upwellings in the Gulf of St. Lawrence, it does keep them high enough to support plenty of copepods for whales who do not mind diving deep for food.

THE BEST PLACE IN THE WORLD TO SEE NORTHERN RIGHT whales is in the Bay of Fundy, in late summer and in autumn. It was here that the species in the North Atlantic Ocean was rediscovered in 1980 by New England Aquarium researcher Scott Kraus and others. Most researchers had thought that whaling had driven them too close to extinction to allow the species to survive.

How did these right whales escape the attention of whalers? Perhaps the Fundy tides kept out whaling ships, creating a natural refuge for the rights. Or perhaps the last of the rights, having hidden for years somewhere in the open recesses of the North Atlantic, discovered the Bay of Fundy only a decade or two ago. In any case, they seem to have adopted the bay: many return year after year. Rights use it as a nursery, a safe place for mothers to bring their calves. For right-whale researchers such as Kraus, it is also the

*Page 71:*
Tides, mysterious and powerful, move to the rhythms of the moon and the sun.
PHOTOGRAPH: WILLIAM ROSSITER

Right whales and right-whale researchers feel at home in the Bay of Fundy. A curious right-whale calf leaves its mother's side to visit the boat. Researcher Amy Knowlton leans over the rail to greet it.

PHOTOGRAPH: GREGORY STONE,
NEW ENGLAND AQUARIUM

place where they bring *their* families. Kraus, his wife, and two young daughters move into research headquarters in nearby Lubec, Maine, each year to observe for a few months the "Fundy kindergarten."

On October 6, it is foggy, but the sea is calm, except for the rip tides of dawn. Stripe and her fat calf, now nearly 28 feet long, double her birth length, chase copepods deep in the water column at the southwest end of the Bay of Fundy. There are about two dozen other right-whale cows and calves, and they are all feeding. Some of the sloppy eaters surface with mud on their faces: they have hit the bottom by accident.

For weeks, Stripe has been demonstrating to the calf how to hyperventilate and take deep breaths in order to feed at deep levels. The deep breaths are needed, as the food is not so close to the surface as it is in Massachusetts Bay and Great South Channel. Now she shows the calf how to navigate the powerful underwater currents created by the Fundy tides—part of the art of turning natural events to one's own advantage.

Swimming upside-down along the 300-foot contour east of Grand Manan Island, Stripe discovers an underwater rock cliff that drops 100 feet to a narrow canyon with a funnel-like opening. Floating at the top of the canyon, Stripe finds that she can hold herself almost stationary in the current, mouth open, and that her meal comes to her as copepods stream through the funnel. Next the calf tries it. Then they take turns floating over the cliff edge, catching the current and the food. Having swallowed the food, they ride the current to the surface, bubbles tickling their skin and, beneath all the blubber, their full bellies. Cracking the surface in unison, they blow and take in sweet, fresh air. They repeat this food-and-fun routine two dozen times. Twice, misjudging the current, Stripe veers off and slams head first into a

Most right-whale mating occurs on Browns Bank, which researchers call "the singles' bar." Sometimes, however, surface active groups form in the Bay of Fundy, usually a nursery for mothers and calves.

PHOTOGRAPH: AMY KNOWLTON,
NEW ENGLAND AQUARIUM

mud patch at the top of the cliff. Her bonnet, the callosity on top of her head, is covered in mud. Then the calf obliges with a mud dunk. Every time the whales surface, the sky is lighter, and finally, the sun burns away the fog. The New England Aquarium researchers motor up slowly in their 29-foot-long fiberglass boat, the *Nereid*, and move in to take a few close-up photographs. Stripe and her calf—with mud on their faces—are not very photogenic. A little tired, they hang at the surface, looking up at Kraus and his team.

For a week, Stripe notices that the air is cooler than in previous days. Her breaths are tinged with autumn, and the water temperature is down. One night, Stripe, without ceremony, leaves her calf and swims across the bay. A half-moon is rising over Fundy, and the sea is calm, except for rip tides that sound like free-flowing waterfalls. The moonlight sparkles on the smooth parts of Stripe's back, making her callosities look like scraggy rocks. The plankton are so thick in the water that Stripe's every tail stroke produces the green glitter of bioluminescence. This light show, a bit of midnight magic, comes from certain species of red-tide phytoplankton that light up like fireflies when disturbed. Stripe passes schools of torch-carrying mackerel and a fat harbor seal that hogs the spotlight. Then a puffing herd of harbor porpoises circle her. Their hyperactive display is like a dozen children waving sparklers at night. Even their spouts of water are green like footlit fountains.

Shortly after dawn, Stripe approaches the Scotian Shelf and chooses to swim by Browns Bank to see what is happening. She finds other right whales midway between Browns Bank and Baccaro Bank, 150 miles southeast of the Bay of Fundy. These rough and wild waters are a long way from the Fundy kindergarten. Kraus calls Browns Bank the "singles' bar" because of the many surface active groups of eligible bachelors, maybe 25, who come here to fight over a few available females.

How available are the females? In the typical right-whale mating ritual, the female calls to the males, then lies on her back on the surface of the water, her vagina inaccessible to would-be suitors. Stripe watches as a female floats on her back and the males push and shove to get next to her. There is no way they can mate when she is on her back, but they want to be ready. She holds her breath, floating on her back for what seems an age. Finally, she must take a breath. She rolls over on her belly and spouts. Before she can even suck in a deep breath, a male on one side of her slides underneath and presses his belly close to hers. The other males push and shove, and at least two 7-foot-long penises unfurl. Yet only the male who managed to get next to her succeeds in copulating. The next time she has to breathe, another male may be victorious. Compared with the aggressive mating ritual of the humpbacks, that of the right whales seems like a free-for-all. Nonetheless, the male who consistently stays close is the one most likely to get his genes into the next generation.

So much promiscuous sex for a species verging on the edge of extinction is encouraging. Apparently, it is also "out of season"—far from any warm-

A right-whale surface active, or courtship, group is a free-for-all of tails and flippers and spinning torsos. As males jockey for position, the female lies on her back playing hard to get.

PHOTOGRAPH: JANE HARRISON,
NEW ENGLAND AQUARIUM

A right-whale calf opens its mouth as it tries to feed. By early autumn, the calf is eating solid food, small crustaceans called copepods. The youngster is now almost 28 feet long, having doubled its birth length.

PHOTOGRAPH: SCOTT KRAUS,
NEW ENGLAND AQUARIUM

water mating ground! Kraus and his team have seen between 7 and 13 new calves in the Bay of Fundy nursery every year. With deaths from natural causes, fishing nets, and ship collisions, however, the right-whale species is doing little more than holding its own. Some researchers wonder whether there are too few northern rights to support a spirited return of the species.

Still watching, Stripe sees a male approaching her. Exhausted from recent motherhood, she just wants to be left alone. She turns and ducks out of sight. In another year, maybe two, she will be ready to mate. She swims south across Browns Bank and into the deep Northeast Channel. On Georges Bank, she finds a good patch of copepods. Then, rolling in the big swells, she lies at the surface—a fat cork bobbing in the sea—and ponders the immediate future of one right whale in the North Atlantic.

Meanwhile, in the Bay of Fundy, Scott Kraus sees Stripe's calf. Kicked out of the nest, she is fine, diving deep and apparently feeding. At nine months, she is on her own, perhaps a little early. Most right-whale calves are on their own by their first birthday. She eats and eats, putting on weight for her first solo migration, now only weeks away. She will be following the others this winter. Maybe Stripe will be there, but it does not matter. The whales remaining in the Bay of Fundy—calves a little older than she, together with a few adults—will travel in a convoy, perhaps swimming along the continental-shelf line. No one will get lost. It will be a long trip, but she will make it.

THE HUMPBACK WHALES OF THE GULF OF MAINE—FRIENDLY Beltane, Talon, her calf, Rush, Comet the singer, and others—are swimming inshore from Great South Channel, along Cape Cod, and into Massachusetts

Bay. It has seemed a freakish past year or two for humpbacks, since the sand lance crashed on their summer home on Stellwagen Bank. They have had to swim long traverses across the gulf, searching for large concentrations of schooling fish—even large patches of krill would have sufficed. They would like more reliability in their source of food. Swimming across Stellwagen Bank, they cannot help but notice the high number of copepods in the water. Sand lance usually feed on copepods, but now basking sharks and sei whales, rarely seen and usually far out at sea, have come in to eat the surplus. Comet and the other humpbacks, however, are not interested in copepods. It is late October, and if anything in the western North Atlantic is reliable, it is the herring run on Jeffreys Ledge, north of Stellwagen Bank.

On the morning of October 16, the humpbacks sweep through the herring schools and gulp tens of thousands of fish at the rate of about one mouthful per minute. The feeding rush lasts six hours, then the herring schools become crafty and disappear. Most of the fish are one-year-old herring, called "brit," that are three to five inches in length—the humpback whales' favorite size. For five days in a row, massive schools of herring hide deep in the water column and wait for darkness to hunt for plankton—the copepods, krill, and other zooplankton on which they depend. Other herring, 10 inches or more, are three- to four-year-old adults that have come to spawn. Each female lays thousands of eggs, which sink to the bottom and stick. With luck, some eggs will hatch in two weeks; others never will. Eventually, the herring's hunger drives the fish to the surface, their silver scales now visible. Day after day, for most of two weeks, the humpbacks, side by side, feast on the herring. In the low light of autumn, the whales lunge and thrust out of the water, creating a primeval scene. Fishermen from Gloucester,

Humpback whales feed in the low light of autumn. One of the surest meals in the Gulf of Maine is the October herring run. With winter close, feeding becomes a little more urgent.

PHOTOGRAPH: JANE GIBBS

Massachusetts, stand at the bow of their boat gaping at the spectacle. On another boat, researcher Mason Weinrich, of the cetacean research unit at the Gloucester Fishermen's Museum, takes identifications, photographing each tail before the whale makes a long dive. In a season of up-and-down feeding, Beltane, Talon, Rush, Comet, Point, and some 15 other humpbacks are not interested in entertaining anyone. Nevertheless, the scene is exciting to watch. Both whales and whale watchers are temporarily sated. Yet many of the whales will stay up north for as long as they can this year, to get enough to eat before they migrate to the Caribbean.

WINTER CREEPS IN EARLY ALONG THE NORTHERN GULF OF ST. Lawrence. First, the grease ice forms, then the pancake ice, floating in the sea slush. Finally, a crust forms—a quarter-inch rind, an inch-thick slab, a foot-thick concrete block. As the ice extends farther and farther from shore and the breathing holes narrow, the blue whale June—eating on borrowed time—prepares to leave the krill-rich upwellings of the north shore of the gulf. Only a few more mouthfuls of that delicious gulf krill. She feeds around the clock, putting on weight, extra fat for the travelling days ahead. It could be months before she eats this well again. Day after day, she postpones the trip. The cold winds gust, and blow snow to the ice edge. At the surface, she feels the sting of the wind, even through her blubber.

Grease and pancake ice are not obstacles. June has only to avoid the clutches of ice that might harden, and trap her, blocking her route to the open sea. She can break through thin ice to create breathing holes. That is the source of some of the blue-whale scars, marks that allow Richard Sears and his research team in the gulf to identify blues easily. Some of the team's favorite whales, Pita, Patches, and Hagar, have ice scars on their backsides, which show up in photographs as a series of vertical gashes. The researchers have never remained in the gulf long enough to see the whales caught in ice. By late November, the researchers are long gone, their inflatable boats packed away, no match for the waters of frozen northern Québec. "You'd need an icebreaker to work this place in winter," says Sears. Some years, however, Sears has returned in an airplane to count the whales that have stayed behind—big, blue would-be icebreakers.

Finally, in early December, June starts moving. She passes other whales on their way out of the gulf before it freezes over. She keeps to the main part of the channel. One night, she surfaces only feet from a freighter that almost hits her. She rolls away in its bow wave. It, too, is leaving the gulf. Montréal, and other ports farther up the St. Lawrence River, will soon be closed to shipping traffic.

June swims out of the gulf through the ice-choked Strait of Belle Isle and follows the ice edge along southern Labrador, navigating the first real blizzard of the season. Surprisingly, the water is almost warm at the surface, though chilling fast from the harsh winds blowing over Labrador. In the Labrador Sea, she finds herself in a cell of water moving to the bottom, a massive vertical current. One of the few areas in the world ocean where cold, deep water is formed, the Labrador Sea can experience unpredictable weather. With all of this water cooling and sinking, new water must come from somewhere else to replace it. If that water flows in from cold Davis Strait, temperatures are going to get even colder. If that water comes from the warm south, then the winter may turn mild. Massive water convection, followed by a great deal of warm water being imported from the south, may lead to warmer winters in the north for several years.

June has no time to waste. Glimpsing the pack ice moving down from Davis Strait, she turns south along Newfoundland's east coast. After six days of steady travelling, she rounds the Avalon Peninsula and, two days later, swims into Cabot Strait, where she entered the gulf with her calf, Junior, last spring. She dives deep, into the "river" of the Laurentian Trough, far below the strait, which separates Newfoundland from Nova Scotia. This water, so cold in summer, seems almost hot now, compared with the surface waters. Swimming toward Newfoundland's southwest coast, she finds other blues she knows feeding. But ice is starting to form here, too.

Days later, the coldest Arctic air mass in recent memory blows out of the north and freezes most of Newfoundland's south-coast bays. The ice edge is marching out to sea. Then, overnight, a bad northeaster pushes in pack ice. The blue-whale feeding grounds are completely blocked. Through the water, June can hear the thundering cries of several blues surrounded by ice. Without a break in the weather, the breathing holes will soon close.

Researchers led by Jon Lien, of Memorial University of Newfoundland, have tried to free blue whales trapped in ice, which usually occurs in late winter or early spring. Since 1958, some 35 blues have been reported stuck off Newfoundland and in the gulf, of which 23 died. Most of the others escaped on their own. Once, a Canadian Coast Guard vessel successfully towed a blue dubbed Reckless Fred across the ice, but the odds of surviving a tow are low.

Three days later, after an unusually warm 24 hours, the ice cracks and splits, and the blues are free. June nudges a young male that reminds her of Junior as the blues turn toward the open North Atlantic. Gaining speed now, they sail off into the clear, blue, dark waters. In a few days, June will meet the warmer eddies of the Gulf Stream. But no human knows where she will go from here. Sears and his research team wish that they knew, but the winter hideout of North Atlantic blues remains one of the great whale mysteries. No one knows whether they even have a common mating ground. Maybe June will swim northeast, toward Norway or Spitsbergen, and try to feed a bit more. Or maybe she will poke around southern Newfoundland but a little farther out, in open waters. Or maybe she will try farther south. No matter, she will soon disappear for the winter, her secret intact.


FAR TO THE SOUTH OF QUEBEC, THE GULF OF MAINE IN LATE autumn is ice free. The humpback whales, having moved from Great South Channel to Massachusetts Bay, at the southern end of the gulf, feel no urgency to leave. Instead, Comet, Beltane, Talon, and Rush want to squeeze in as many meals as they can before the long winter fast and the fun begins on the mating grounds.

Unlike rights and especially blues, humpbacks are sociable and often feed close together. Rush, nearly a year old, is lunge-feeding, having learned how to eat by watching his mother, Talon, and her friends. Talon does not seem to mind having him around, and he may even tag along when she and the others start migrating. It may be more out of habit than out of need: Rush is now largely self-sufficient. Some humpback calves accompany their mothers on the migration south to the mating grounds, then return to the feeding grounds with them the following spring, perhaps spending as long as a year and a half together. Another new calf, Tatters, is on his own. His mother, Scylla, has already left on migration, but he has stayed to feed with some of his summer companions.

Life could hardly seem better for humpbacks, at least since the end of the whaling era in the early 1970s. The humpback population is in much better shape than that of blues and rights. Some researchers believe that the humpbacks may be coming back in number and repopulating their old haunts. They sing and mate in the Caribbean in January and February. They cruise the open sea in March and April. They visit Bermuda. By late April or early May, they have reached the summer resorts of Cape Cod, Maine, New Brunswick, Nova Scotia, Newfoundland, and Québec. Throughout the summer and into autumn, they take all the seafood they can eat. But life in the sea is not always all it seems.

THEY COME OUT OF THE NORTH, DARK SHADOWS UNDER-water, great schools swimming tightly packed, skimming the surface like thousands of tiny black missiles, racing around the southern tip of Nova Scotia and heading into the Gulf of Maine. Mackerel. Wide-ranging and somewhat unpredictable roamers, northern mackerel spend their summers in the Gulf of St. Lawrence, where they spawn. They feed widely on zooplankton. They are not choosy: they take whatever they can find. Swimming through the Gulf of Maine, the mackerel are on their way to warmer, offshore waters in the North Atlantic where they like to go in winter. They do not expect to run into hungry humpback whales along the way. Humpbacks, at least in this part of the world, do not eat much mackerel.

But this year, one strange environmental occurrence seems to lead to another. In the gray days of late November, Beltane, Talon, Comet, and Tatters are among the humpbacks who decide to stay a few more weeks around Cape Cod before they migrate south, to the Caribbean. They are hungry. The mackerel swim into Massachusetts Bay, and the excited humpbacks charge through the massive schools, mouths open, gorging themselves. In a matter of hours, Beltane, leading the group, eats a few thousand pounds of fish. Her usual daily feed may be 3,000 to 4,000 pounds. That evening, she and several other mature females eat a few thousand more. In the morning, mackerel is the entrée again, with several other fishes and some krill as side dishes. By mid-afternoon, Beltane and some of her companions are feeling sick. Could it be what they ate? Or could it be something else—perhaps a manmade chemical, a bacteria, or a virus? What could lay low a 40-ton whale?

Beltane swims around and around, exhausted. She feels hot, then cold. Every 10 minutes, she has the urge to swim fast and to breach clear of the water. That evening, blinded by the pain, she has trouble breathing. She leaves the others, some of whom are also feeling a little sick, and swims out to

A humpback whale leaps, a dark silhouette on a brooding sea.

PHOTOGRAPH: CENTER FOR COASTAL STUDIES

sea, as if to try to catch the migration.

On the morning of November 28, the telephone rings at the wood-frame house on Commercial Street in Provincetown, Massachusetts, where the Center for Coastal Studies has its headquarters. On the line is the U.S. Coast Guard. A dead whale, "could be a humpback," is floating offshore. Center researchers Phil Clapham and Lisa Baraff ride out with the Coast Guard. The dead animal turns out to be a minke whale.

Three hours later, in the afternoon, there is another call. The tide has brought a dead whale to Thumpertown Beach, at Eastham, in Cape Cod Bay. Jumping into his car, Clapham drives a few miles down the cape to investigate.

Walking along the beach, he sees that this whale is indeed a humpback. It looks strangely familiar. Clapham goes right for the tail, the clue to most humpbacks' identities. It looks like Beltane, but the animal is so big, partly as a result of the bloating after death. The animal has been dead for at least two days. Yet even in death, the whale looks healthy and robust, a 45-foot-long female in the prime of life. He hopes that it is not Beltane, the whale who gave researchers the first third-generation humpback calf. He has known Beltane since she was born in 1980. Along with Talon, she supplied him with the data he needed for his paper that announced that humpback females can reach sexual maturity as young as age four.

Clapham returns to the laboratory and examines the file photographs of humpback tails. The dead whale is definitely Beltane. What could have happened? The whales that strand around Cape Cod are usually toothed whales, especially pilot whales, not baleen whales, such as humpbacks. In 10 years, only three humpbacks beached themselves on Cape Cod.

The Coast Guard agrees to tow Beltane to Provincetown for tests. The necropsy tells the researchers from the New England Aquarium and the Center for Coastal Studies that Beltane died quickly and that she had a stomach full of mackerel. But it does not reveal the cause of death.

Ten days later, on December 8, a humpback calf washes up on Beach Point, in Truro, just south of Provincetown. It is Scylla's calf, Tatters. Tatters, as well, is full of mackerel. Clapham is sad but knows that calf mortality at the end of the first year is not unheard of. Three years earlier, Binoc's calf stranded on Cape Cod.

On December 12, Carole Carlson is driving into Provincetown, on her way back from the Marine Mammal Conference in Miami, Florida. The long-time center researcher, now working with the International Wildlife Coalition of Falmouth, Massachusetts, thinks about how nice it is out on the water, flat calm, and wishes that she could go out. She has heard about the two dead humpbacks. When she arrives at the center, another report comes in. In minutes, she is in a Zodiac inflatable boat and out on the water. A big male humpback is floating near Long Point, off Provincetown. He is bloated, his belly up. There are pebbles caught in his pleats, as if he already washed up on a beach somewhere, then rolled off. One of the center's research ships, the *Halos,* tows the humpback to shore. The white streak across the otherwise all-black underside of his tail is unmistakable. It is Comet. The ugly reptilian singer will sing and fight no more. As he lays there so still and vulnerable,

Carlson feels her loss welling up inside. "Here he is on this beach I've walked along and lived beside for so many years," she muses, "an old friend, dead, and about to be cut up." For weeks to come, Comet will stay there, rotting. Every time Carlson looks out in her "backyard," she feels as if she is having a recurring nightmare.

In the necropsy, conducted on the beach, Comet, too, proves healthy, with a stomach full of mackerel, including one whole 15-inch-long fish still in his mouth. For the first time, Phil Clapham considers that the humpback deaths, now three, may be more than coincidence and that "something may be wrong out there." There may be some major problem with the whales' environment, some swift, silent killer.

Clapham begins to coordinate a field effort. He sends the whole mackerel in Comet's mouth—along with samples of mackerel from local fishermen—to the Woods Hole Oceanographic Institution for analysis. With center researcher Jeff Goodyear, Carole Carlson starts taking plankton samples in Cape Cod Bay. These, too, are sent to Woods Hole.

A 30-foot-long male humpback whale comes ashore. Before 1987, this was a rare event around Cape Cod.
PHOTOGRAPH: CENTER FOR COASTAL STUDIES

A humpback-whale calf washes in on the tide to a Cape Cod beach. Humpbacks, except for calves, rarely strand. Researcher Carole Carlson has tender words for Binoc's calf.

PHOTOGRAPH: CENTER FOR
COASTAL STUDIES

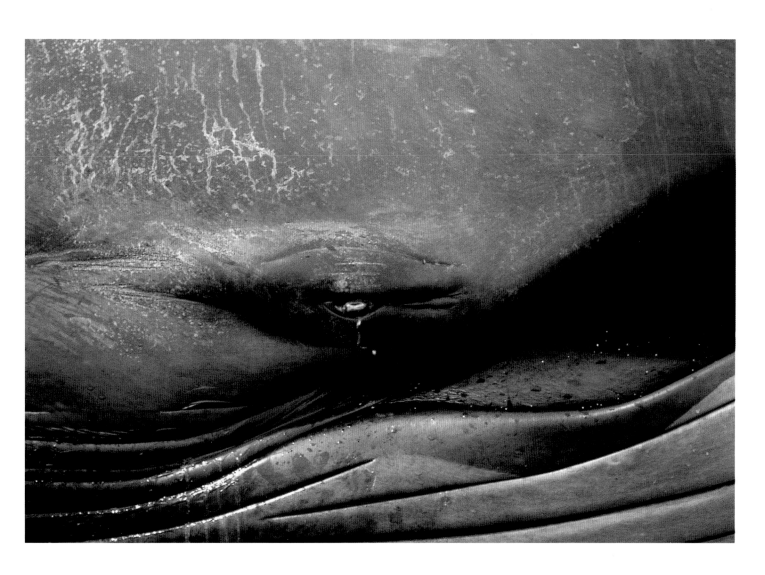

A tear falls from the eye of a dying whale.
PHOTOGRAPH: CENTER FOR
COASTAL STUDIES

On December 14, a 41-foot-long mature female humpback washes up dead on the incoming tide at Fisher Beach, in Truro. It is Point. Seen every year since 1979 off Cape Cod, Point was twice a mother—in 1985 and 1987. Her calf of the year is nowhere to be seen.

The next day, Carlson watches a humpback die. In the morning, she is standing on the beach beside the dead Point when a humpback just offshore starts breaching and splashing. At first, she thinks that it may be Point's calf coming to look for his mother. But it turns out to be Torch, a 33-foot-long male. Torch is feeding and breaching. Then his movements become so frenetic that Carlson knows he cannot be jumping for joy. In the early afternoon, when she and Goodyear motor out in the Zodiac to collect more plankton samples, young Torch is still there, breaching and thrashing. The other whales she sees are feeding. The mackerel are skipping across the water, almost dancing on their tails, and the whales are lunging at a 45-degree angle, a third of their bodies in the air, their mouths open and gulping.

Carlson and Goodyear ride farther out to sea in the Zodiac. Ninety minutes later, as the center's ship, the *Halos,* approaches off Truro, Torch rolls on his side and dies. The boat tows the half-bloated whale to Provincetown, to the beach where Comet lies so silent.

The International Wildlife Coalition flies an aerial survey the same day. To everyone's horror, two more dead humpbacks are found on the cape—Tuning Fork, a 40-foot-long female, and an unknown whale.

On December 17, high tides bring two more whales to Cape Cod beaches: a small male named Ionic to East Dennis and an unknown 33-foot-long female to North Beach, near Chatham, on the outside of the cape. She is the first whale to strand in an area exposed to the open North Atlantic. As the possible area of stranding expands by an order of magnitude, what has seemed a local event may be much bigger. Newspapers from *The New York Times* to the Toronto *Globe and Mail,* as well as television news shows, begin to cover the story, some providing daily death tolls. *The Boston Globe* gives it the front page for several days in a row. With nine humpback whales stranded in three weeks, reporters want to know what is wrong, and researchers such as Carole Carlson and Phil Clapham feel the pressure to come up with an answer.

One researcher suggests that the whales might have died from red-tide organisms. The name "red tide" comes from the reddish color of the seawater, produced by large numbers of red phytoplankton called "dinoflagellates." But not all red tides are red, and they actually have nothing to do with tides. These massive plankton "blooms" occur usually in summer. They are caused by a number of factors that center on the sudden availability of nutrients in the water, from excess river run-off into the sea after heavy rains, from warmer than usual temperatures, or even from closeness to sewage outflows. Through the action of bacteria, certain red-tide organisms, the dinoflagellates, produce a toxin. When some fish eat enough of the dinoflagellates, they die. Other fishes, shellfish, and zooplankton survive but, when eaten themselves, send the toxin up the food chain to humans and perhaps even to whales.

A pilot whale strands in the marsh grass of Cape Cod. In December 1986, about 60 pilot whales washed ashore, many of them alive. Some were pushed back out to sea, but most died on the beach. Three young males, however, were rescued by the New England Aquarium, rehabilitated, and returned to the wild.

PHOTOGRAPH: CENTER FOR
COASTAL STUDIES

But, the researcher cautions, it is only a wild theory. Red tides have come and gone in the ocean environment for a long time, probably long enough for whales to have evolved a way of dealing with them. Indeed, whales have never been known to be affected by red-tide toxins. Furthermore, the plankton samples collected by Carlson and Goodyear off Provincetown do not contain red-tide toxins.

The mystery of the deaths deepens day by day as more and more whales die. Every whale researcher on the East Coast is talking about the tragedy and eager to do anything to help.

Scott Kraus, now in Boston following his fieldwork with right whales in the Bay of Fundy, climbs into a plane and flies out to sea, to run transections to scout for whales. Researchers are concerned that there may be more floating dead out there. Kraus worries about his right whales, too. Some have not yet headed south. If this high a death toll had hit right whales with their low numbers, it would have driven them closer to extinction. Kraus makes a mental note to check contaminant levels in right-whale tissues, to start to gather some baseline data in case rights suffer a humpback-type disaster in the future.

Even Richard Sears, from his research station on the north shore of the Gulf of St. Lawrence, more than 500 miles away, begins to wonder whether blue whales have been affected. Two blues stranded in the gulf during the season, one in May on Anticosti Island, near Sears's station, and the other in October on Prince Edward Island. Sears and his team did not recognize either whale. The cause of death was also unknown.

Sears now recalls that a red-tide bloom occurred during the summer in the Gulf of St. Lawrence. The toxin turned up in shellfish, especially mussels. There were 37 cases of human poisoning in Canada. So far away from Massachusetts Bay, yet could there be a connection? What about the bottlenose dolphins dying since midsummer farther to the south? By the end of the year, they are still dying, though the weekly totals have fallen. The main stranding area is almost 500 miles south of Cape Cod, along the coast of Virginia. None have stranded north of New Jersey. Initially, no whale researcher believes that the mass deaths of humpbacks and dolphins are connected, though a few begin to wonder what is going wrong in the North Atlantic. Nevertheless, Joseph Geraci, the researcher in charge of the investigation into the dolphin deaths, takes a short leave to study the dead humpbacks. The scientific effort needs every marine-mammal pathologist it can get.

On December 18, Massachusetts Department of Public Health officials announce that a red-tide toxin has been found in the livers of the mackerel the dead humpbacks had been eating. Two questions, however, remain unanswered: Could a red-tide toxin from a microscopic plant be carried by mackerel without the mackerel themselves dying? Could such a toxin be powerful enough to bring down a whale? It still seems unlikely. Meanwhile, public-health officials caution people against eating any mackerel until further tests are done. There have been no red-tide episodes in the Gulf of Maine that year. Could the mackerel have eaten something offshore or farther north?

The search proceeds. Researchers look for a route a toxin may take through the ecosystem, from phytoplankton to giant whales. They look for

A blue whale lands on the beach in Prince Edward Island in 1987—cause of death unknown. The same year, another blue strands on Anticosti Island, in the northern Gulf of St. Lawrence.

PHOTOGRAPH: WAYNE BARRETT

other factors. As Christmas approaches, dead whales continue to wash ashore. On December 22, two more humpbacks, Rune and K, are found, as well as an unknown whale out at sea, on Nantucket Island. On December 29, the thirteenth whale lands on a beach. It has been dead for two weeks. As the difficult year ends, east-coast whale researchers tentatively celebrate the new year, hoping that the strandings are finally over, that the tides will not bring any more surprises.

Day by day, in the short, dark days of December, Talon plows through the water, feeding to make up for the time she lost in her first year as a mother. She has watched some of her summer companions die in recent weeks, but she does not know why. Rush, her calf, remains with her, tired of feeding weeks ago and still waiting for his mother to finish so that they can join the migration trains that pass daily—trains of whales from the far-northern feeding grounds off Greenland and Newfoundland.

But Talon is sluggish. Her aggressive open-mouthed skirmishes through the mackerel schools are getting slower and slower. She stops eating. Rush thinks that she is just resting. He swims around her. Then Talon lurches forward, swimming fast, as if to play. She races around as if she were on fire. She breaches again and again. She slaps her 15-foot-long flippers from side to side. She smacks her tail on the surface, asking all to witness her death. Rush remembers the behavior of Comet and Beltane.

As the toxin takes hold of Talon, she screams in pain. She can no longer breathe. The pressure is intense in her brain, her muscles, her lungs—through her whole being. Finally, she surrenders and lets her body fall. Rush tries to support her. But Talon is falling—100 yards, 300, 600, the telltale white wings spinning slowly into the black depths. Rush dives deep with her, for as far as he can hold his breath. Then he swims back to the surface. Talon is gone.

For a few hours, days it seems, Rush stays by the patch of rolling sea where his mother disappeared. Then he must leave. He feels queasy for a few days but hangs on, breathing deeply.

On January 3, Talon's corpse, badly bloated from the gases of putrefaction, rises to the surface. The incoming tide brings her gently onto a beach near Provincetown where, hours later, someone sees her and calls the Center for Coastal Studies. Phil Clapham, who has examined most of the dead whales, drives down to Race Point, his chest tightening. Walking down the beach toward the carcass, he wonders, "Who the hell will it be this time?"

At first, the tail looks like that of Talon's sister, one of Sinestra's other calves, a few years younger. But another researcher, Mason Weinrich, points out the L-shaped mark on the tail—Talon's "claw." "It's definitely Talon," he says. Stunned, just standing there, Clapham realizes how numb he has become over the whole tragedy. For seven weeks, he has done nothing but "look for dead whales, find dead whales, tow dead whales, cut up dead whales, try to dispose of dead whales, deal with the press on dead whales, deal with the public on dead whales, deal with religious fanatics writing in and telling us that they could tell us why the whales were dying, that it is all a part of an act of God."

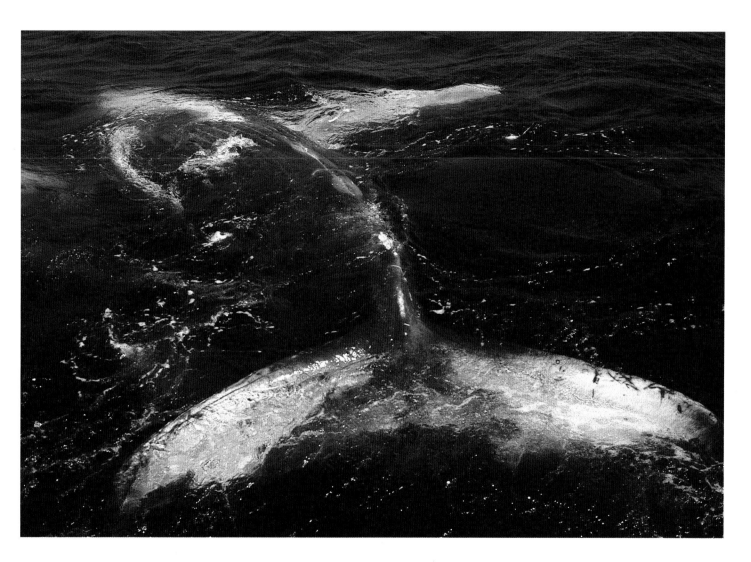

A humpback whale, on her back just below
the surface, sinks into the black.

PHOTOGRAPH: JANE GIBBS

Clapham almost does not care who strands anymore. He has become resigned to losing "a reasonable portion of the population." With Talon, however, it all cracks. Her death is the crushing blow. As she lies there so still, Clapham's thoughts race back to so many happy times with her. Talon was seen day in and day out for seven years since her birth, both on the feeding grounds at Stellwagen Bank and on the mating grounds in the Caribbean. He remembers Talon as a calf playing around the research vessel or entertaining a Portuguese family out in a small boat while her often-standoffish mother, Sinestra, remained on the sidelines. He remembers the time he and some other researchers threw a float in the water and Talon played with it. He remembers Talon's curiosity and what seemed like pride when she showed them her new calf, Rush, only months ago.

Later that day, a friend from the center calls Carole Carlson, who has returned to Dalhousie University, in Halifax, Nova Scotia, where she is writing her Ph.D. The friend tells her to sit down. Carlson's master's research was on Talon and the way her tail patterns had changed since birth; her Ph.D. research was on the behavior of Talon and other whales. More than that, Carlson had a personal connection with Talon, her favorite whale. Now there is a pause on the telephone line as her friend tells of Talon's death. As Carlson grasps what has happened, she feels the shock. She will never see Talon again.

The humpback whales left behind in the winter migration of 1987–88 will live on in the memory of those who saw their leaps and spins over the North Atlantic.

PHOTOGRAPH: CENTER FOR
COASTAL STUDIES

A few days later, southeast of Cape Cod, Rush joins some fellow survivors who are travelling south. The long feeding season is over. But there is much to look forward to on the humpback mating and calving grounds of the Caribbean. Somehow they recognize that life must be renewed. Whales, the grandest form of life ever known, seem to fight stoically against this one more tragic episode. Heading out to the edge of the continental shelf, Rush and the others meet more humpbacks swimming south from Newfoundland, Nova Scotia, and the Gulf of St. Lawrence. Blowing, breathing, and diving, they move rhythmically in a line, a grand procession that celebrates life. This year, the migration to the Caribbean does not include Comet, Beltane, Point, or Talon. Instead, these whales live on in the memories of those who heard their songs or saw their leaps and spins over the cool North Atlantic.

A survivor, Sinestra, mother of Talon, was photographed a few months after the 1987–88 humpback-whale deaths around Cape Cod. She has since been seen with a new calf.

PHOTOGRAPH: WILLIAM ROSSITER

# POSTSCRIPT
April 1990

IN TWO OR THREE DECADES, people have gone from killing whales to trying to save them. Today, as more and more people join the ranks of whale watchers, the survival of whales has become a matter of personal concern for the lives of individual animals.

The big blue whales June, Kits, Pita, Backbar, and Hagar have been seen since 1987 and are all doing well. Junior has not been sighted, but he may have found new feeding grounds, off Iceland or Greenland.

The clumsy right whale Stripe and her various calves are all accounted for. Her daughter Stars still has the rope looped around her jaw but seems fine. The other rights appear healthy, continuing their slow climb back from the edge of extinction.

Of the humpback whales, Talon's calf, Rush, has not been seen since 1987, but he, too, may have chosen a new feeding ground in the North Atlantic Ocean, perhaps off Greenland, where researchers rarely go. For the most part, life on the humpback feeding grounds in the Gulf of Maine has returned to normal. Most of the humpbacks who stayed away from Stellwagen Bank following the sand-lance crash of 1986 and 1987 have returned to that area. Talon's mother, Sinestra, survived and in 1988 appeared with a new calf. Beltane's calf, Cat Eyes, is doing well, as is Beltane's mother, Silver, who was seen in 1989 with yet another new calf. Point's calf, born in 1987, may have been sighted, but whale researchers have only a photograph of a dorsal fin.

In all, 14 humpback whales were found dead around Cape Cod between late November 1987 and early January 1988—7 males and 7 females, including 1 calf. During the same period in that area, 2 fin and 3 minke whales also washed ashore. Researchers do not know how many more whales died, and floated far out to sea or stranded on some piece of remote coast. They may not know for several years, until the familiar ones are missed. About 5 percent of the Gulf of Maine population of an endangered species is dead, however, and researchers admit that the real figure may be closer to 10 percent.

Did the red-tide toxin in the mackerel kill the 14 humpback whales? There was extensive research conducted by Joseph Geraci, Donald Anderson, and others from the Center for Coastal Studies, the Woods Hole Oceanographic Institution, the New England Aquarium, and the University of Guelph in Ontario. Their studies built a strong case that the culprit was a red-tide toxin called "saxitoxin." This toxin was never found in the whales themselves, but extracts from several of the humpbacks' stomachs and organs had toxic properties. Some nagging questions remain: Why did some mackerel-eating whales die and others apparently did not? Was it simply a case of how much they ate?

The best explanation for the deaths is as follows: The mackerel picked up the red-tide toxin in the Gulf of St. Lawrence in the summer or early autumn and retained it in their livers during their annual migration to the Gulf of Maine. There, perhaps weakened by the toxin, they were easy prey for hungry humpbacks. The humpbacks ate mackerel voraciously during the autumn in Massachusetts Bay because their usual food, sand lance, was unavailable. It may not take much toxin to kill a whale. Humpbacks are 30 percent blubber. The water-soluble saxitoxin would bypass blubber and concentrate in physiologically sensitive tissues in the heart and the brain. A dose that might give humans temporary muscle fatigue or even hypothermia *could* kill a whale. Humans have automatic breathing and other systems that "take over"; they also have medical care. But a whale needs to be conscious and physically fit to stay warm and to come to the surface to breathe.

After the red-tide diagnosis for humpbacks was reached, Joseph Geraci returned to the investigation into the bottlenose-dolphin deaths with new insights. In March 1988, nine months after the first dolphin stranded on the New Jersey coast, the mass dolphin deaths ended. Altogether, more than 740 dolphins were found dying or dead from New Jersey to Florida, about half of the coastal population. The humpback deaths led Geraci to search for a red-tide organism to explain the dolphin deaths, even though the condition of the animals, the timing, the place, and the species were all different.

On February 1, 1989, after 17 months of research, Geraci held a press conference with the National Oceanic and Atmospheric Administration, the U.S. government agency sponsoring the study. As principal investigator, Geraci declared that the bottlenose dolphins had died of poisoning from eating fish carrying a red-tide toxin. The fish—menhaden—had picked up the toxin in the Gulf of México, then carried it to the east coast of the U.S., where the dolphins began feeding on them. The guilty toxin was brevetoxin—a different red-tide toxin than that which appears to have killed the humpbacks. But both are red-tide toxins that occur naturally in the ocean environment.

The outcome of the study surprised many of the journalists, whale researchers, and conservationists at the press conference. "You mean pollution had nothing to do with it?" asked one journalist. "Nothing!" Geraci replied. It was difficult to ask probing questions without a copy of the report or the background data. Geraci admitted that more work needed to be done, but whale researchers such as Carole Carlson, Marine Mammal Stranding Center director Bob Schoelkopf, and Greenpeace consultant Bruce McKay were annoyed that so little attention was being given to the possible role of pollution "at a time when we need to be looking into it."

Some weeks later, after the report was released, Congress called a special hearing in Washington, D.C. On May 9, 1989, Geraci, nervous in the spotlight, met his critics, a panel of other marine-mammal researchers. Among them were Pierre Béland and Daniel Martineau, of the St. Lawrence National Institute of Ecotoxicology in Québec. In sum, the panel said that Geraci had drawn his conclusions from too few toxin samples while dismissing an overwhelming amount of information on manmade pollutants. According to Geraci, brevetoxin was found in 8 of 17 dolphin carcasses, in 1 fish in the stomach of a dolphin, and in 3 fish caught off Florida. Béland and Martineau, drawing on their work with belugas, suggested that organochlorine compounds such as PCBs may have played an important role in the deaths. Unlike the 14 stranded humpbacks, all robust and otherwise healthy animals, the dolphins had been covered in lesions—the kind found on animals intoxicated with PCBs—and had died slowly. The dolphins had also suffered from severe septicemia, accompanied by bacteria. That meant that their immune systems had been suppressed—another sign of PCBs.

Geraci had found extraordinarily high levels of organochlorines in the dolphins, among the highest ever found in marine mammals. Yet he had downplayed their importance. Béland said that the presence of PCBs in the liver, more than in the blubber, is alarming. Most likely, he said, the dolphins had recently eaten fish contaminated with PCBs, banned in the United States since 1979 but still in the environment. Once weakened, and perhaps in combination with the brevetoxin or other contaminants, the dolphins died en masse.

But there are some unexamined possibilities. In his first released draft of the report, Geraci wrote that a remarkably high number of animals had washed ashore with respiratory difficulties like those contracted from inhaling a toxic irritant. In the final report, this information was dropped without explanation. The red-tide brevetoxin could produce a toxic seaspray aerosol but only from the plankton bloom itself, not from the fish that carried the brevetoxin. Thus, the effect in air would not likely extend beyond Florida to New Jersey or even the Carolinas and Virginia, where most of the strandings occurred. When the first dolphins found on the beach in New Jersey had fluid build-up in the lungs characteristic of toxic gas, Bob Schoelkopf promptly notified the federal government through the National Marine Fisheries Service. As well, many beachgoers to the New Jersey coast during midsummer 1987 complained of respiratory problems. Yet the federal government never ordered an investigation or a test of the air quality offshore.

Schoelkopf, however, later met with the U.S. Army's chemical warfare group in Maryland. They were concerned about their offshore disposal units of mustard gas and other chemicals. Some of the gas had been dumped off Florida, and two ships carrying chemicals had gone down in the northeast, one about 200 miles off Atlantic City, New Jersey. The chemicals were housed in steel-cased drums not designed for long-term storage at sea.

After the congressional hearing, several congressmen, along with Greenpeace, called for reopening the investigation. Now, almost three years after the dolphins started stranding, the request is still pending, and no one knows for certain why the dolphins died. Nevertheless, there has been one positive outcome of the dolphin and humpback strandings and the ensuing controversies. People, governments, and scientists are on the alert. The State of New Jersey, for example, recently set up a crack team of "green police" to bust illegal dumpers and polluters. The team has 29 plain-clothes officers, 13 lawyers, and a budget of $2 million. It will take time for scientific research to get a handle on coastal pollution and its effects. But the days are numbered for continued use of the ocean as a cheap and convenient way to dispose of industrial waste and sewage sludge, as the bottomless dump of the planet.

What is the future of the ocean, this ecosystem on which whales and dolphins, their fish, krill, and copepod prey, and we humans depend? Whales and dolphins are the most visible animals in the ocean realm. They are also among the most susceptible to pollution. They travel great distances in a year, from industrial coastlines to deep-sea trenches, into bays, and even up certain rivers. Feeding at or near the top of the food chain, they can pick up toxins or contaminants from their prey or the prey of their prey, and the evidence tends to concentrate and remain in their organs and tissues. Thus, whales and dolphins are valuable because they can tell us when things are not right in the sea. In 1987, the long string of beached deaths along the East Coast issued an eloquent, if at times harsh, warning of how fast a toxin or contaminant can move through the food chain. Was it a foretelling of the future if we do not listen? The whales can only hope that we are paying attention.

PHOTOGRAPH: INTERNATIONAL FUND
FOR ANIMAL WELFARE

# SOURCES

Anderson, Donald M., and Alan W. White (eds.). "Toxic Dinoflagellates and Marine Mammal Mortalities." Proceedings of an Expert Consultation Held at the Woods Hole Oceanographic Institution. Woods Hole Oceanographic Institution Technical Report, WHOI-89-36 (CRC-89-6), Nov. 1989, pp. 1–65.

Carson, Rachel. *The Edge of the Sea*. Boston: Houghton Mifflin, 1955, pp. 1–276.

Clapham, Phillip J., and Charles A. Mayo. "Reproduction and Recruitment of Individually Identified Humpback Whales, *Megaptera novaeangliae*, Observed in Massachusetts Bay, 1979–1985." *Canadian Journal of Zoology*, vol. 65, pp. 2853–2863.

Geraci, Joseph R. "Clinical Investigation of the 1987–88 Mass Mortality of Bottlenose Dolphins Along the U.S. Central and South Atlantic Coast." Final Report to National Marine Fisheries Service; U.S. Navy, Office of Naval Research; and Marine Mammal Commission, Apr. 1989, pp. i–ii, 1–63.

———, Donald M. Anderson, Ralph J. Timperi, David J. St. Aubin, Gregory A. Early, John H. Prescott, and Charles A. Mayo. "Humpback Whales Fatally Poisoned by Dinoflagellate Toxin." *Canadian Journal of Fisheries and Aquatic Sciences*, vol. 46, 1989.

Hoyt, Erich. *The Whale Watcher's Handbook*. Garden City, New York: Doubleday; Toronto: Penguin/Madison Press, 1984, pp. 1–208.

———. "Masters of the Gulf. Life Among the Whales of the St. Lawrence." *Equinox*, vol. 4, no. 3, May–June 1985, pp. 52–65.

———. "New England's Harried Harbor Porpoise: Scientists Are Studying a Little-Known Marine Mammal Threatened by Commercial Fishing Gillnets." *Defenders*, vol. 64, no. 1, Jan.–Feb. 1989, pp. 10–17.

Katona, Steven K., Valerie Rough, and David T. Richardson. *A Field Guide to the Whales, Porpoises and Seals of the Gulf of Maine and Eastern Canada: Cape Cod to Newfoundland*. New York: Charles Scribner's Sons, 1983, pp. i–xvi, 1–256.

Kraus, Scott D., John H. Prescott, Amy R. Knowlton, and Gregory S. Stone. "Migration and Calving of Western North Atlantic Right Whales (*Eubalaena glacialis*)." In Best, Peter B., Robert Brownell, and John H. Prescott (eds.). *Report of the Workshop on the Status of Right Whales*. Reports, International Whaling Commission, Special Issue No. 10, 1986.

Leatherwood, Stephen, Randall R. Reeves, and Larry Foster. *The Sierra Club Handbook of Whales and Dolphins*. San Francisco: Sierra Club Books, 1983, pp. 1–302.

Lien, Jon. "Problems of Newfoundland Fishermen with Large Whales and Sharks During 1987 and a Review of Incidental Entrapment in Inshore Fishing Gear During the Past Decade." *The Osprey*, vol. 19, nos. 1 and 2, 1988, pp. 30–38, 65–71.

McKay, Bruce. "Fish Story: The Government Says 750 Dolphins Died of Food Poisoning. But No One's Biting." *Greenpeace*, vol. 14, no. 4, July–Aug. 1989, pp. 12–13.

O'Hara, Kathryn, Natasha Atkins, and Suzanne Iudicello. *Marine Wildlife Entanglement in North America*. Washington, D.C.: Center for Environmental Education, 1986, pp. i–iv, 1–219.

Orlean, Susan. "On the Right Track: Counting Whales in the Bay of Fundy." *The Boston Globe Magazine,* Nov. 27, 1983, pp. 10–11, 30–36.

Payne, Roger, and Scott McVay. "Songs of Humpback Whales." *Science,* vol. 173, 1971, pp. 585–597.

Robbins, Sarah F., and Clarice M. Yentsch. *The Sea Is All About Us.* Salem, Massachusetts: The Peabody Museum of Salem and The Cape Ann Society for Marine Science, Inc., 1973, pp. 1–162.

Rowntree, Victoria. "Cyamids: The Louse that Moored." *Whalewatcher,* vol. 17, no. 4, Winter 1983, pp. 14–17.

Sears, Richard. "Photo-identification of Individual Blue Whales." *Whalewatcher,* vol. 18, no. 3, Fall 1984, pp. 10–12.

————, Frederick W. Wenzel, and J. Michael Williamson. *The Blue Whale: A Catalogue of Individuals from the Western North Atlantic (Gulf of St. Lawrence).* St. Lambert, P.Q.: Mingan Island Cetacean Study (MICS Inc.), 1987, pp. 1–27, P1–P56.

Stone, Gregory S., Steven K. Katona, and Edward B. Tucker. "History, Migration and Present Status of Humpback Whales *Megaptera novaeangliae* at Bermuda." *Biological Conservation,* vol. 42, 1987, pp. 133–145.

Stutz, Bruce. "Last Summer at the Jersey Shore: A Plague of Problems—And a Rash of Answers." *Oceans,* July–Aug. 1988, pp. 8–14, 65.

# INDEX

LIBRARY
ST. LOUIS COMMUNITY COLLEGE
at FOREST PARK
ST. LOUIS, MISSOURI